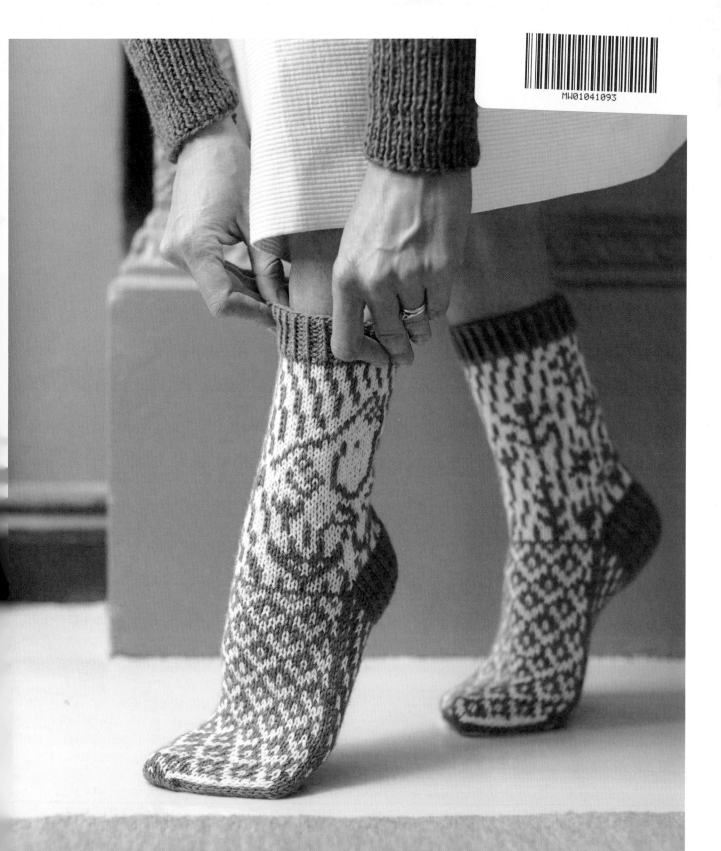

KNITTED MOOMIN SOCKS

First published in Great Britain 2024 by
Search Press Limited
Wellwood, North Farm Road,
Tunbridge Wells, Kent TN2 3DR

© Moomin Characters™
Published in English by arrangement with
Rights & Brands.
English translation by Burravoe Translation Services

Editor: Linda Permanto
Contributor: Paula Nivukoski
Designers: Pirjo Iivonen, Marita Karlsson,
Minna Metsänen, Sonja Nykänen, Sisko Sälpäkivi
and Minttu Wikberg
Knitting patterns: Jaana Etula
Photography: Roope Permanto
Location: Punkaharju Hotel, South Savo, Finland
Photographed knits: Novita, www.novitaknits.com
Graphic design and layout: Venla Koski and
Päivi Puustinen

ISBN: 978-1-80092-177-1
ebook ISBN: 978-1-80093-166-4

All rights reserved. No part of this book, text,
photographs or illustrations may be reproduced or
transmitted in any form or by any means by print,
photoprint, microfilm, microfiche, photocopier, video,
internet or in any way known or as yet unknown, or
stored in a retrieval system, without written permission
obtained beforehand from Search Press.
Printed in China.

The Publishers and contributors can accept no
responsibility for any consequences arising from
the information, advice or instructions given in
this publication.

Readers are permitted to reproduce any of the items in
this book for their personal use, or for the purposes of
selling for charity, free of charge and without the prior
permission of the Publishers. Any use of the items for
commercial purposes is not permitted without the
prior permission of the Publishers.

Suppliers
If you have difficulty in obtaining any of the materials
and equipment mentioned in this book, then please
visit the Search Press website for details of suppliers:
www.searchpress.com

Bookmarked Hub
For further ideas and inspiration, and to join our free
online community, visit www.bookmarkedhub.com

FSC
www.fsc.org

MIX
Paper | Supporting
responsible forestry
FSC® C016973

KNITTED MOOMIN SOCKS

29 original designs with charts

Inspired by the works of Tove Jansson

Contents

The Hemulen Collecting Flowers 14

Berry Picking 20

Dancing in the Rain 26

Happy Sniff 32

Flowers for the Snorkmaiden 38

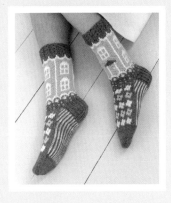

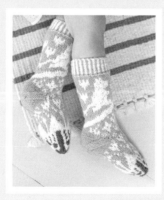

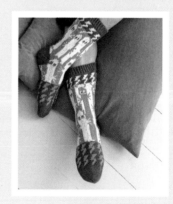

'And over the floor two woollen socks came waddling and laid themselves down before Moomintroll.'

Moominland Midwinter

Foreword

Dear sock knitter,

Adventure might be just around the corner. It starts in the corner of the sofa, in the pages of a book. When you're journeying to foreign lands and exciting tomorrows, book in hand, it's essential your toes don't get chilly.

Sometimes the journey takes you far away down narrow paths. Step by step, you wander into unfamiliar territory, sensing the right place to put your feet on slippery rocks. Once you have reached your destination, you unpack your provisions and rest for a while.

Everyone can always do with comforting words and comforting socks. Pop a pair of knitted socks in your rucksack even on a summer's evening. That way, when the night starts to get chilly as you sit outside watching the sun go down, you won't have to cut the moment short because your feet are cold. Linger on with a friend, toes touching! Let the world settle into place, and watch the sun set and rise.

A night in late autumn might find you dancing, sock-footed, on a jetty by a lake; lighting lanterns in the dark; and then happily padding across the grass before tiptoeing quietly to bed and snuggling down to sleep.

On a winter's morning, wake and run across the crunchy snow. Wool socks keep the snow out and the warmth in.

Anyone given socks knitted with love will be overjoyed. Amazing ideas, tender moments and hopes of future adventure are entwined into every knitted stitch. Whether you pad silently to your own room or launch out into the big wide world, with warm socks on your feet it's like taking a hug with you wherever you go.

Paula Nivukoski

Author of the Moomin ABC books

Are you motherly and gentle like Moominmamma?

Or small and fierce like Little My? We wanted to make this knitted sock book for all of you who have found your inner Moomin and gained joy, comfort and wisdom from Tove Jansson's wonderful characters.

This book contains 29 unique sock patterns created by top Finnish knitwear designers inspired by Tove Jansson's wonderful world. Designing these detailed colourwork patterns took a lot of imagination and technical skill. Making each set of instructions easy to understand is also an art form in itself. Knitting should be relaxing and fun, not a headache.

The 29 gorgeous socks in this book are knitted using the Moomin x Novita range of yarn. These yarns bear the Key Flag symbol, showing that they are Made in Finland.

For this book we needed a unique photography location, the kind of place you might find in the world of the Moomins – somewhere that lives and breathes warmth while buzzing with life, the natural world and history. We found it in Finland's lake district, in the magical beauty of the Punkaharju Hotel in South Savo.

We are grateful to everyone involved in making this book. Thank you for joining us in creating this fabulous fairy-tale sock book. You can almost hear footsteps in warm knitted socks as you turn the pages.

Knitted socks – more of a gift than a garment.

Linda Permanto

Editor

Socks for Moomin fans of all sizes

BE BRAVE AND ADAPT THE INSTRUCTIONS

We wanted to keep all kinds and all sizes of feet warm, from Mymble to the Groke and from baby to grandad. The instructions in this book come with suggested shoe sizes but all the instructions can be modified to fit any size of foot. So, don't despair if your favourite Moomin design isn't in the size you want.

The main part of the sock is mostly knit in a Fair Isle design, which you need to bear in mind when thinking about fit. Fair Isle isn't as stretchy as stocking (stockinette) stitch in one colour, so Fair Isle socks don't give you as much wiggle room (literally). On the other hand, the pattern of a Fair Isle sock will last well from one wear to the next. On this page you'll find advice on how to change the size of your sock with the patterns in this book in mind. Remember to work a tension (gauge) swatch first! (See page 120.)

CHANGE NEEDLE SIZE

The socks in this book are close-fitting on the leg, designed for a narrow calf. If you want a roomier sock, you can knit the pattern using larger needles. In the same way, you can make the sock narrower by working on smaller needles. This may be necessary when making socks for children. It's up to you whether you change needles for the whole sock or just for the Fair Isle section.

This way of changing the size will work for all the sock patterns. It's especially handy for patterns with a more challenging Fair Isle design and where changing the number of stitches will have too great an impact on the pattern. For example, you could make the Rambling Roses socks (page 90) smaller or larger by changing needle size.

CHANGE THE NUMBER OF STITCHES OR ROUNDS IN STOCKING (STOCKINETTE) STITCH

Besides changing the needle size, perhaps the easiest way of changing the size of your sock is to shorten or lengthen sections worked in one colour in stocking (stockinette) stitch. In some of the patterns in this book, the foot is worked partly or completely in one colour. These include Sonja Nykänen's lovely A Summer's Day socks (page 118) or Pirjo Iivonen's delicate Primadonna's Horse socks (page 96). When you're working a single-colour foot, you can knit as many rounds as you need to get the length you want. It's worth remembering though that you need to start decreasing for the toe once the sock covers the future wearer's little toe.

To change the width, again you will need to increase or decrease the number of stitches. Work a few more gusset decreases and your sock will fit a narrower foot. To make the calf wider, again you will need to add more stitches. For example, Marita Karlsson's snuggly The Invisible Child socks (page 86) can be made wider by adding stitches in the background colour on either side of the Fair Isle panel. Remember to decrease these extra stitches when you get to the heel.

ADD OR REDUCE THE NUMBER OF PATTERN REPEATS

A handy way of changing the size in Fair Isle patterns is to add or reduce pattern repeats, if the design allows. Of course you can do this widthwise or lengthwise. Working repeats to the length needed is part of the instructions, for example in Minttu Wikberg's inspired Berry Picking socks (page 20) and Mymble's Herb Garden socks (page 44). In these patterns, the Fair Isle design is repeated as often as necessary.

Dive into the world of Moomin-inspired socks and don't be afraid of changing the sizing to make your knitted socks perfect.

Happy knitting!
The Novita pattern design team

Checking your tension (gauge)

All the patterns start by stating the tension (gauge). This means it's important to first knit a swatch and check that you are knitting to the same tension (gauge) as in the instructions. If your knitting is tighter or looser, your socks won't be the same size as stated in the pattern.

KNITTING A SWATCH

First, knit a swatch using the same yarn, needles and technique stated in the sock pattern. Make the swatch both wide and long enough that you can count the stitches and rows in an area measuring 10cm (4in) square. Place the swatch on a flat surface and steam lightly to block. Place pins to mark 10cm (4in) widthwise and lengthwise. Count the number of stitches and rows within this.

When measuring the tension (gauge) of rib, stretch the swatch slightly when counting the stitches, as with additional rows of rib the garment will be looser. This way, your knitting won't end up too big.

GETTING YOUR TENSION (GAUGE) RIGHT

If your swatch doesn't come out the same tension (gauge) as stated in the pattern, change your tension (gauge) by changing the size of your needles. If your swatch has too few stitches per 10cm (4in), i.e. your knitting is too loose, change to smaller needles. If your swatch has too many stitches per 10cm (4in), your knitting is too tight and you need larger needles.

Always work a new swatch to check you have got your tension (gauge) right and that your end result will be the right size. Remember that if you use a different yarn from the yarn stated in the instructions, you may need more or less yarn than that stated.

YARN

All the socks in this book use yarns in the Moomin x Novita range: Muumitalo (Moomin House) and Muumihahmot (Moomin Characters). Huviretki (Adventure) yarn knits up to the same tension (gauge) but because of its composition, it can't withstand heavy wear and so isn't recommended for the feet of socks.

Abbreviations

alt = alternate
k = knit
p = purl
LH = left hand
sl = slip
skpo = slip 1 stitch knitwise, knit 1 in working yarn and pass the slipped stitch over the knitted stitch
ssk = slip, slip knit (slip 2 stitches onto the right-hand needle, slide the stitches back on to the left-hand needle and knit them together through the back loops)
st = stitch
st st = stocking (stockinette) stitch
RH = right hand
RS = right side
WS = wrong side
– = repeat from * to *

Sock measurement table

Shoe size UK	Shoe size Europe	Shoe size US women's	Shoe size US men's	Shoe size US children's	Sock (cuff) circumference	Leg sts
Child's 5	22			C6	16cm (6¼in)	40
Child's 8½	26			C9½	18cm (7in)	44
Child's 11½	30			C12½	20cm (7¾in)	48
1½	34	4	2½		22cm (8¾in)	52
5	38	7½	6		24cm (9½in)	56
8	42	10½	9		26cm (10¼in)	60
11	46	13½	12		28cm (11in)	64

To work to a smaller shoe size than those listed above, begin the decreases a few rounds earlier. To work to a larger shoe size, work a few additional rounds before beginning the increases. Make sure that any alterations will not impact the colourwork.

Heel flap sts and rows	Division of heel sts for heel decrease	Sts picked up from edge of heel flap	Length of foot before toe decreases	Length of whole foot
20	6+8+6	10+1	12cm (4¾in)	15cm (6in)
22	7+8+7	11+1	13cm (5in)	17cm (6¾in)
24	8+8+8	12+1	15cm (6in)	20cm (7¾in)
26	8+10+8	13+1	17cm (6¾in)	22cm (8¾in)
28	9+10+9	14+1	20cm (7¾in)	25cm (9¾in)
30	10+10+10	15+1	22cm (8¾in)	28cm (11in)
32	10+12+10	16+1	25cm (9¾in)	31cm (12¼in)

THE HEMULEN COLLECTING FLOWERS

The leg of this sock, designed by Marita Karlsson, shows the Hemulen gathering flowers. Using the ladder back jacquard technique keeps the Fair Isle pattern even, avoiding long floats on the wrong side. The socks have a ribbed cuff, a reinforced heel and a wedge toe.

DESIGNER Marita Karlsson

SIZES UK 5/6(6½/7½) (Europe 38/39(40/41), US Women's 7½/8½(9/10), US Men's 6/7(7½/8½))

YARN

2 balls of Novita Muumitalo (Moomin House) DK (8-ply/light worsted) yarn in Moomintroll 007 (A) and 1 ball each in Hemulen 720 (B) and Snufkin 381 (C); 100g/3½oz/225m/246yd

AMOUNT USED

200g (7oz) of yarn A, 100g (3½oz) of yarn B and 50g (1¾oz) of yarn C for both sizes

KNITTING NEEDLES

3mm (UK 11, US 2/3) double-pointed needles or size to obtain correct tension (gauge)

TECHNIQUES

Twisted rib in the round:
knit 1 through back loop, purl 1, repeat from * to *.

Stocking (stockinette) stitch in the round:
Knit all rounds

Fair Isle in the round:
Work in stocking (stockinette) stitch following chart and instructions. Catch in any floats longer than 4 sts by twisting the yarns around each other at the back of the work. Vary where you catch your floats in the design so they don't land in the same place on consecutive rounds. Use the ladder back jacquard technique to catch in floats on the leg. You can find videos and instructions showing how to do this online.

TENSION (GAUGE) 29 sts in Fair Isle = 10cm (4in)

NOTE

The socks are worked top down from cuff to toe.

RIGHT SOCK

Cast on 80(84) sts in yarn C and divide between four needles as follows: 26(28) sts on needles I and IV and 14(14) sts on needles II and III. The start of the round is between needle I and needle IV at the back of the sock.

Join, being careful not to twist, and work 4.5cm (1¾in) in twisted rib in the round. Break yarn.

Start the Fair Isle pattern, working round 1 of Chart I A across all 80(84) sts. Then work rounds 2–70 of chart. Decrease at places marked on chart. **Note:** when following the instructions for the larger size, always treat the decrease st for the smaller size as a knit st and work it in the yarn as shown by the colour of the square.

Break off yarns B and C and work 6cm (2¼in) in stocking (stockinette) stitch in yarn A.

Divide sts evenly with 13(14) sts on each needle.

HEEL

Start to work heel by knitting the sts on needle I on to needle IV (26(28) sts for heel flap). Leave remaining sts on needles II and III. Turn work and start slip stitch pattern to reinforce heel:

Row 1 (WS): sl1 (with yarn at back of work), purl to end of row. Turn work.

Row 2 (RS): *sl1 (with yarn at back of work), k1*, repeat from * to * to end of row. Turn work.

Repeat rows 1 and 2 a total of 13(14) times and then work row 1 again (27(29) rows).

Start to work a French heel (rounded heel):

Row 1 (RS): sl1 (with yarn at back of work), k14(15), ssk, k1. Turn work.

Row 2 (WS): sl1 purlwise, p5, p2tog, p1. Turn work.

Row 3: sl1 knitwise, k6, ssk, k1. Turn work.

Row 4: sl1 purlwise, p7, p2tog, p1. Turn work.

Continue decreasing in this way, increasing the number of sts in the centre by one on each row until all sts at the sides have been decreased. Then work one more WS row. **Note:** for the larger size, there will be no stitch left to k1/p1 at the end of the row after the last decrease.

Turn work. Divide heel sts evenly between two needles with 8 sts on each needle. Knit sts on RH needle. This point (centre back) is now the start of the round.

FOOT

Knit the 8 sts on LH needle from heel (needle I). Using a spare needle, pick up 14(15) sts from LH edge of heel flap + 1 st between heel flap and needle II. Knit picked up sts on to needle I, turning sts knitwise. Knit sts on needle II and needle III. Using the needle with 8 sts on it, pick up 14(15) sts from RH edge of heel flap + 1 st between heel flap and needle III. Knit picked up sts and 8 sts from heel on to needle IV, turning picked up sts knitwise. You now have 72(76) sts.

Continue in stocking (stockinette) stitch, decreasing for gusset as follows: k2tog at end of needle I and ssk at beginning of needle IV. Repeat decreases on every alternate round until there are 13(14) sts left on each needle.

After the gusset decreases, continue in stocking (stockinette) stitch for about 5cm (2in) and then start the Fair Isle pattern at round 1 of Chart II A (Chart III for larger size). Work all rounds of chart.

Continue in stocking (stockinette) stitch in yarn A until the foot of the sock measures approximately 20.5(22)cm / 8(8¾)in or covers the wearer's little toe.

Start to decrease to work a wedge toe:

Needle I and needle III: work to last 3 sts, k2tog, k1.
Needle II and needle IV: k1, ssk, work to end.

Decrease as set on every alt round until there are 36 sts left and then work decreases on every round until there are 16 sts left.

Continued overleaf.

Chart I A

Work rounds 1–70

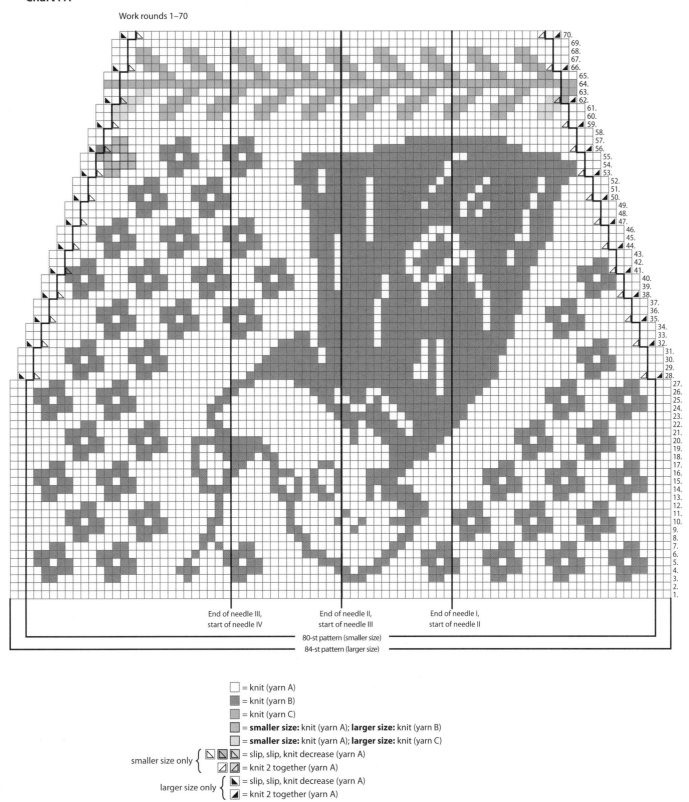

End of needle III,
start of needle IV

End of needle II,
start of needle III

End of needle I,
start of needle II

80-st pattern (smaller size)
84-st pattern (larger size)

☐ = knit (yarn A)
■ = knit (yarn B)
▨ = knit (yarn C)
▨ = **smaller size:** knit (yarn A); **larger size:** knit (yarn B)
▨ = **smaller size:** knit (yarn A); **larger size:** knit (yarn C)

smaller size only ⎰ ◺ ◺ ◺ = slip, slip, knit decrease (yarn A)
⎱ ◿ ◿ = knit 2 together (yarn A)

larger size only ⎰ ◣ = slip, slip, knit decrease (yarn A)
⎱ ◢ = knit 2 together (yarn A)

17

Chart I B

Work rounds 1-70

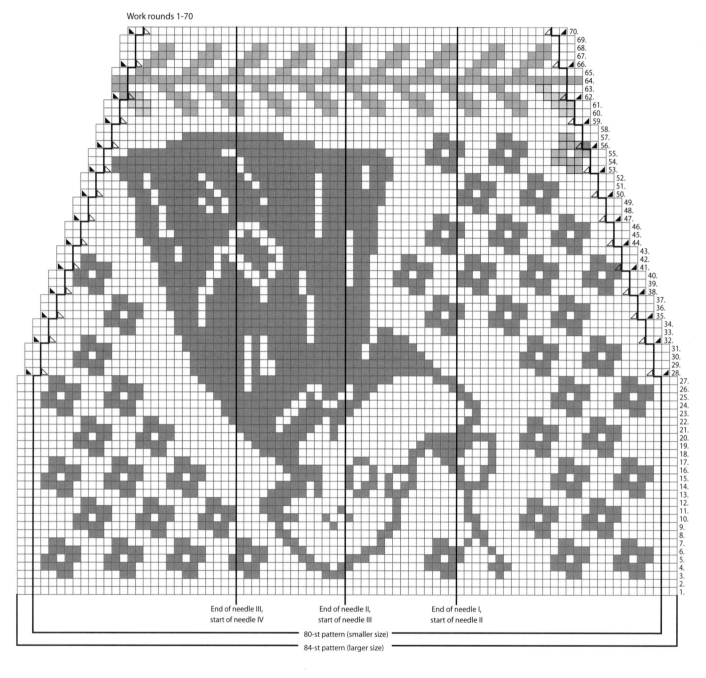

End of needle III,
start of needle IV

End of needle II,
start of needle III

End of needle I,
start of needle II

80-st pattern (smaller size)

84-st pattern (larger size)

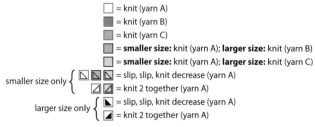

☐ = knit (yarn A)

◼ = knit (yarn B)

◼ = knit (yarn C)

◼ = **smaller size:** knit (yarn A); **larger size:** knit (yarn B)

◻ = **smaller size:** knit (yarn A); **larger size:** knit (yarn C)

smaller size only { ◺◺◺ = slip, slip, knit decrease (yarn A)
◹◹ = knit 2 together (yarn A)

larger size only { ◣ = slip, slip, knit decrease (yarn A)
◢ = knit 2 together (yarn A)

Divide remaining sts evenly between two needles with 8 sts on the upper needle and 8 sts on the lower needle. Graft sts together. There are instructions and videos available online showing how to graft (sometimes called Kitchener stitch).

LEFT SOCK

Work left sock in the same way but using Chart I B for the leg. For the smaller size, use Chart II B for the Fair Isle design on the foot. For the larger size, the Fair Isle pattern on the foot is worked using Chart III (the same for both socks).

FINISHING

Weave in ends. Carefully wet socks, place on a flat surface and block to measurements. Leave to dry. Steam block lightly if necessary.

☐ = knit (yarn A)
▨ = knit (yarn B)

Chart II A

Work rounds 1–11

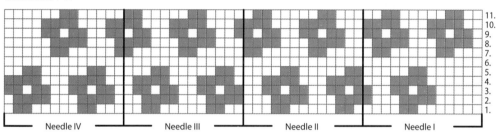

Chart II B

Work rounds 1–11

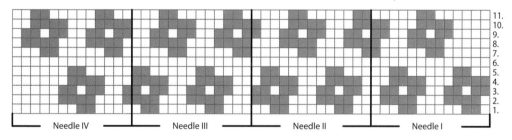

Chart III

Work rounds 1–11

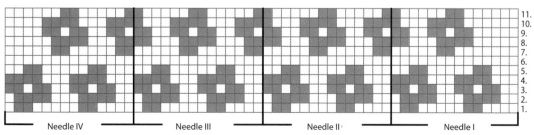

19

BERRY PICKING

Two-colour rib brightens up these socks that show Moominmamma picking tempting red berries, which Moominmamma is going to turn into delicious berry juice. A traditional reinforced heel and a barn toe make these socks practical and a neat fit.

DESIGNER Minttu Wikberg

SIZE UK 5/6 (Europe 38/39, US Women's 7½/8½, US Men's 6/7)

YARN

1 ball each of Novita Muumitalo (Moomin House) DK (8-ply/light worsted) yarn in Miffle 229 (A), The Groke 176 (B), Moomintroll 007 (C) and Fillyjonk 599 (D); 100g/3½oz/225m/246yd

AMOUNT USED

25g (1oz) of yarn A, 50g (1¾oz) of yarns B and D and 100g (3½oz) of yarn C

KNITTING NEEDLES

3mm (UK 11, US 2/3) double-pointed needles or size to obtain correct tension (gauge)

TECHNIQUES

Two-colour rib in the round:
k1 in yarn A, p1 in yarn C, repeat from * to *.

Stocking (stockinette) stitch in the round:
Knit all rounds.

Fair Isle in the round:
Work in stocking (stockinette) stitch following chart and instructions. Catch in any floats longer than 4 sts by twisting the yarns around each other at the back of the work. Vary where you catch your floats in the design so they don't land in the same place on consecutive rounds.

TENSION (GAUGE) 25 sts in st st = 10cm (4in)

NOTE

The socks are worked top down from cuff to toe. Embroider the red details on the leg in duplicate stitch once the sock is complete, copying rounds 1 and 2 of Chart II.

LEG

Cast on 56 sts in yarn A and divide between four needles with 14 sts on each needle. The start of the round is between needle I and needle IV at the back of the sock.

Join, being careful not to twist, and work 3cm (1¼in) in two-colour rib in the round. Change to yarn B and knit one round.

Start the Fair Isle pattern, working round 1 of Chart I A across all 56 sts. Then work rounds 2–45 of chart. **Note:** embroider the red details on the leg in duplicate stitch once the sock is complete.

HEEL

Start to work heel by knitting the sts on needle I on to needle IV using yarn B (28 sts for heel flap). Leave remaining sts on needles II and III. Turn work and start slip stitch pattern to reinforce heel:

Row 1 (WS): sl1 (with yarn at back of work), purl to end of row. Turn work.

Row 2 (RS): *sl1 (with yarn at back of work), k1*, repeat from * to * to end of row. Turn work.

Repeat rows 1 and 2 a total of 14 times and then knit one row (29 rows).

Start to decrease to turn the heel:

Continue in the same slip stitch pattern as before to reinforce heel. Starting with a RS row, work in pattern until there are 10 sts left on LH needle, skpo and turn work.

Sl1 purlwise and purl 8 sts on WS until there are 10 sts left on LH needle. P2tog and turn work.

Sl1 knitwise, work in pattern until there are 9 sts left on LH needle, skpo and turn work.

■ = knit (yarn B)
□ = knit (yarn C)
Ⅴ = embroider sts in duplicate stitch in yarn D once sock is complete

Chart I A

Work rounds 1–45

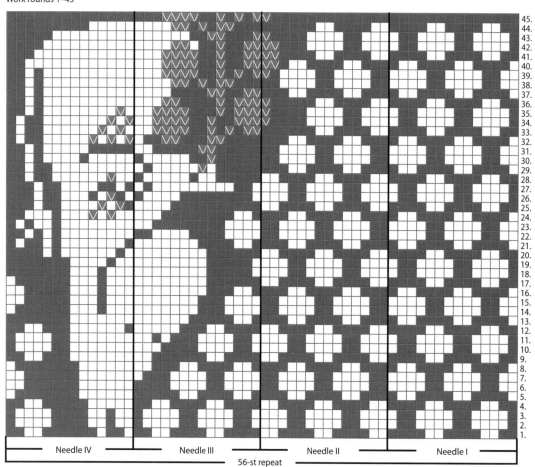

45.
44.
43.
42.
41.
40.
39.
38.
37.
36.
35.
34.
33.
32.
31.
30.
29.
28.
27.
26.
25.
24.
23.
22.
21.
20.
19.
18.
17.
16.
15.
14.
13.
12.
11.
10.
9.
8.
7.
6.
5.
4.
3.
2.
1.

├─── Needle IV ───┤├─── Needle III ───┤├─── Needle II ───┤├─── Needle I ───┤
56-st repeat

Continue as set working back and forth, i.e. always slip the first st of the row and skpo at the end of a RS row and p2tog at the end of a WS row. The number of sts at the sides will decrease by 1 each time, always leaving 10 sts in the centre. When you run out of side sts at the end of a WS row, k5 on RS. This point (centre back) is now the start of the round.

FOOT

Knit 5 sts on LH needle from heel (needle I). Using a spare needle, pick up 14 sts from LH edge of heel flap + 1 st between heel flap and needle II. Knit picked up sts on to needle I, turning sts knitwise. Knit sts on needle II and needle III. Using the needle with 5 sts on it, pick up

14 sts from RH edge of heel flap + 1 st between heel flap and needle III. Knit picked up sts and 5 sts from heel on to needle IV, turning picked up sts knitwise. You have now worked round 1 of Chart II A and have 68 sts.

Break off yarn B and knit 1 round in yarn C (= round 2 of Chart II A). **Note:** the red berry sts on rounds 1 and 2 are embroidered on top using duplicate stitch once the socks are complete.

Continue following Chart II A from round 3, starting to decrease for gusset at the same time as follows: k2tog at end of needle I and skpo at beginning of needle IV. Work this decrease on every alt round until there are 56 stitches left, 14 on each needle. Work chart to the end.

Chart I B

Work rounds 1–45

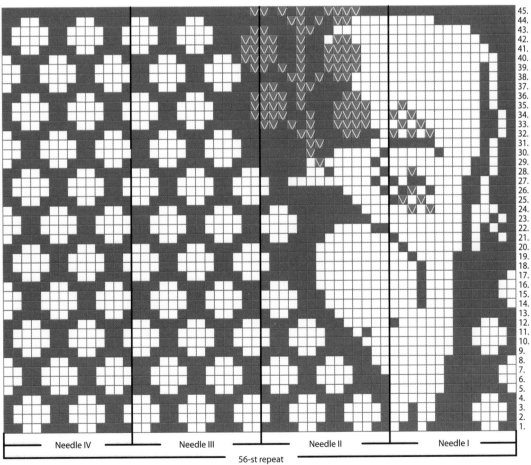

You can repeat rounds 34–41 of Chart II A until the foot of the sock measures about 19cm (7½in) or until the foot covers the wearer's little toe. Then continue in yarn A and start to decrease for the toe.

Note: don't start to work a new berry on the last round. If you are in the middle of a berry, complete it as you work the toe decreases. Then finish the rest of the sock in yarn A.

Decrease to work a barn toe as follows:

Needle I and needle III: work to last 3 sts, k2tog, k1.
Needle II and needle IV: k1, skpo, work to end.

Decrease as set on every alt round until there are 40 sts left and then work decreases on every round until there are 8 sts left. Break yarn and thread through remaining sts.

SECOND SOCK
Work other sock as a mirror image following Charts 1 B and II B.

Chart II A

Work rounds 1–41

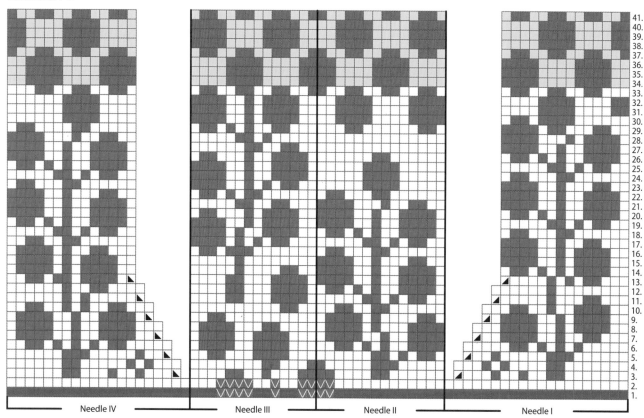

= knit (yarn B)

= knit (yarn C)

= embroider sts in duplicate stitch in yarn D

= knit (yarn D)

= knit (yarn A)

= knit 2 together (yarn C)

= slip 1 stitch knitwise, knit 1 in yarn C and pass the slipped stitch over the knitted stitch

FINISHING

Embroider the red details as shown on Charts I and II using duplicate stitch.

Weave in ends. Carefully wet socks, place on a flat surface and block to measurements. Leave to dry. Steam block lightly if necessary.

Chart II B

Work rounds 1–41

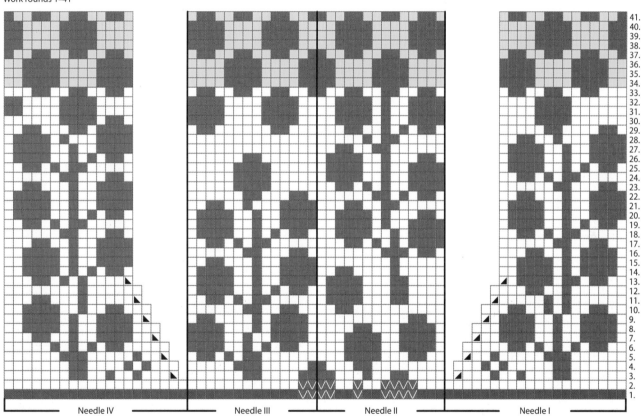

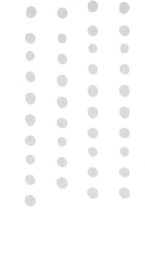

DANCING IN THE RAIN

Here Moomintroll is dancing in the rain. These fun blue-and-white knitted socks are close-fitting and best suit adults with small feet, or children of school age. The knit stitches in the rib at the top are twisted.

DESIGNER Minttu Wikberg

SIZE UK 1½ (Europe 34, US Women's 4, US Men's 2½)

YARN

1 ball each of Novita Muumitalo (Moomin House) DK (8-ply/light worsted) yarn in The Groke 176 (A), Moomintroll 007 (B), and Snork 152 (C); 100g/3½oz/225m/246yd

AMOUNT USED

100g (3½oz) of yarn A, 50g (1¾oz) of yarn B and 25g (1oz) of yarn C

KNITTING NEEDLES

3mm (UK 11, US 2/3) double-pointed needles or size to obtain correct tension (gauge)

TECHNIQUES

Twisted rib in the round:
knit 1 through back loop, purl 1, repeat from * to *.

Stocking (stockinette) stitch in the round:
Knit all rounds.

Fair Isle in the round:
Work in stocking (stockinette) stitch following chart and instructions. Catch in any floats longer than 4 sts by twisting the yarns around each other at the back of the work. Vary where you catch your floats so they don't land in the same place on consecutive rounds.

TENSION (GAUGE) 25 sts in st st = 10cm (4in)

NOTE

The socks are worked top down from cuff to toe. Embroider Moomintroll's outline and eye with duplicate stitch on the finished socks following the instructions.

LEG

Cast on 50 sts in yarn A and divide between four needles with 13 sts on needles I and III and 12 sts on needles II and IV. The start of the round is between needle I and needle IV at the back of the sock.

Join, being careful not to twist, and work 3cm (1¼in) in twisted rib in the round. Then knit 3 rounds.

Chart I

Work rounds 1–3

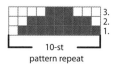

```
      10-st
  pattern repeat
```

■ = knit (yarn A)
□ = knit (yarn B)

Start Fair Isle pattern following round 1 of Chart I and repeating the 10-st pattern five times. Then work rounds 2 and 3 of chart. On last round of Chart I, increase 2 sts evenly in the yarn B part of the design (52 sts). Divide sts equally with 13 sts on each needle.

Start working the 52-st Fair Isle pattern from round 1 of Chart II A. Then work rounds 2–37 of chart. Use yarns B and C only on rounds 1–36. The Moomintroll outline and Moomintroll's eye are embroidered on to the finished sock afterwards.

Then work rest of sock in yarn A.

Chart II A

Work rounds 1–37

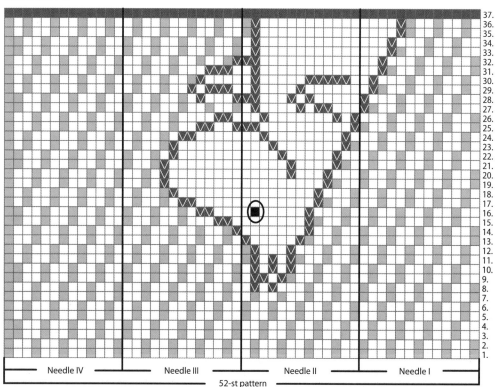

▦ = knit (yarn C)
□ = knit (yarn B)
Ⅴ = embroider sts in duplicate stitch in yarn A
■ = knit (yarn A)
■ = embroider a French knot in yarn A
╱ = embroider in backstitch in yarn A

HEEL

Start to work heel by knitting the sts on needle I on to needle IV (26 sts for heel flap). Leave remaining sts on needles II and III. Turn work and start slip stitch pattern to reinforce heel:

Row 1 (WS): sl1 (with yarn at back of work), purl to end of row. Turn work.

Row 2 (RS): *sl1 (with yarn at back of work), k1*, repeat from * to * to end of row. Turn work.

Repeat rows 1 and 2 a total of 13 times and then knit 1 row (27 rows).

Start to decrease to turn the heel:

Continue in the same slip stitch pattern as before to reinforce heel. Starting with a RS row, work in pattern until there are 10 sts left on LH needle, skpo and turn work.

Sl1 purlwise and purl 6 sts on WS until there are 10 sts left on LH needle. P2tog and turn work.

Sl1 knitwise, work in pattern until there are 9 sts left on LH needle, skpo and turn work.

Continue as set working back and forth, i.e. always slip the first st of the row and skpo at the end of a RS row and p2tog at the end of a WS row. The number of sts at the sides will always decrease by 1, always leaving 8 sts in the centre. When you run out of side sts, k4 on RS. This point (centre back) is now the start of the round.

Chart II B

Work rounds 1–37

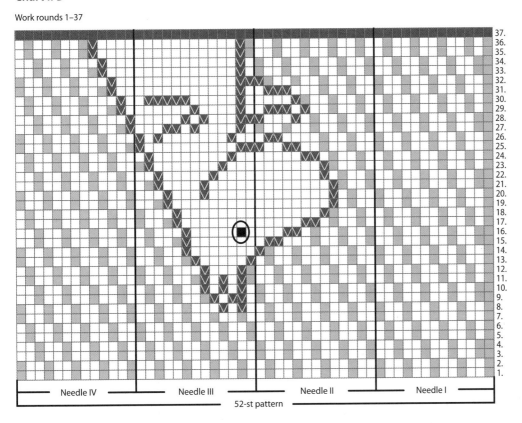

FOOT

Knit 4 sts on LH needle from heel (needle I). Using a spare needle, pick up 13 sts from LH edge of heel flap + 1 st between heel flap and needle II. Knit stitches picked up from edge of heel flap on to needle I through back loops. Knit sts on needle II and needle III. Using the needle with 4 sts on it, pick up 13 sts from RH edge of heel flap + 1 st between heel flap and needle III. Knit picked up sts and 4 sts from heel on to needle IV, turning picked up sts knitwise. You now have 62 sts.

Continue in stocking (stockinette) stitch, decreasing for gusset as follows: k2tog at end of needle I and skpo at beginning of needle IV. Work this decrease on every alt round until there are 52 sts left, 13 on each needle.

Work in stocking (stockinette) stitch until the foot of the sock measures approximately 17cm (6¾in) or until the foot of the sock covers the wearer's little toe.

Continue in stocking (stockinette) stitch and start to decrease to work a barn toe:

Needle I and needle III: work to last 3 sts, k2tog, k1.
Needle II and needle IV: k1, skpo, work to end.

Decrease as set on every alt round until there are 20 sts left and then work decreases on every round until there are 8 sts left. Break yarn and thread through remaining sts.

SECOND SOCK

Work other sock in the same way following Chart II B for the leg.

FINISHING

Embroider the outline around Moomintroll on top of the knitted sts in yarn A using duplicate stitch. Divide a strand of yarn A in two and use to embroider short backstitches around the eye. Create the pupil by embroidering a French knot in yarn A.

Weave in ends. Carefully wet socks, place on a flat surface and block to measurements. Leave to dry. Steam block lightly if necessary.

> "'It's only the rain," said Moomintroll. "The rain has come at last. Now we'll sleep for a bit.'"
>
> *Finn Family Moomintroll*

HAPPY SNIFF

These long socks show Sniff, surrounded by dancing coins, as he loves gold, shiny things. The long floats at the back of the Sniff character can be caught in traditionally or using the ladder back jacquard technique. In terms of fit, these Sniff socks work best for narrow calves.

DESIGNER Marita Karlsson

SIZES UK 5/6(6½/7½) (Europe 38/39(40/41), US Women's 7½/8½(9/10), US Men's 6/7(7½/8½))

YARN

2 balls of Novita Muumitalo (Moomin House) DK (8-ply/light worsted) yarn in Snufkin 381 (A); 100g/3½oz/225m/246yd

2 balls of Novita Huviretki (Adventure) DK (8-ply/light worsted) yarn in Beach 652 (B); 50g/1¾oz/112m/122yd

AMOUNT USED

200g (7oz) of yarn A and 100g (3½oz) of yarn B for both sizes

KNITTING NEEDLES

3mm (UK 11, US 2/3) double-pointed needles or size to obtain correct tension (gauge)

TECHNIQUES

Twisted rib in the round:
knit 1 through back loop, purl 1, repeat from * to *.

Stocking (stockinette) stitch in the round:
Knit all rounds.

Fair Isle in the round:
Work in stocking (stockinette) stitch following chart and instructions. Catch in any floats longer than 4 sts by twisting the yarns around each other at the back of the work. Vary where you catch your floats in the design so they don't land in the same place on consecutive rounds. You could use the ladder back jacquard technique to catch in the long floats in the Fair Isle pattern on the leg. You can find videos and instructions showing how to do this online.

TENSION (GAUGE) 29 sts in Fair Isle = 10cm (4in)

NOTE

The socks are worked top down from cuff to toe.

RIGHT SOCK

Cast on 80(84) sts in yarn A and divide between four needles as follows: 26(28) sts on needles I and IV and 14(14) sts on needles II and III. The start of the round is between needle I and needle IV at the back of the sock.

Join, being careful not to twist, and work 4.5cm (1¾in) in twisted rib in the round. Knit 1 round, decreasing 1 st at start of round (k2tog) and end of round (ssk) (78(82) sts).

Start the Fair Isle pattern, working round 1 of Chart I across all 78(82) sts. Then work rounds 2–89 of chart. Decrease at places marked on chart. **Note:** when following the instructions for the larger size, always treat the decrease st for the smaller size as a knit st and work it in the yarn as shown by the colour of the square.

Break off yarn B and work rest of sock in yarn A. Knit 4 rounds in stocking (stockinette) stitch.

Divide sts evenly with 13(14) sts on each needle.

HEEL

Start to work heel by knitting the sts on needle I on to needle IV (26(28) sts for heel flap). Leave remaining sts on needles II and III. Turn work and start slip stitch pattern to reinforce heel:

Row 1 (WS): sl1 (with yarn at back of work), purl to end of row. Turn work.

Row 2 (RS): *sl1 (with yarn at back of work), k1*, repeat from * to * to end of row. Turn work.

Repeat rows 1 and 2 a total of 13(14) times and then work row 1 again (27(29) rows).

Start to work a French heel (rounded heel):

Row 1 (RS): sl1 (with yarn at back of work), k14(15), ssk, k1. Turn work.

Row 2 (WS): sl1 purlwise, p5, p2tog, p1. Turn work.

Row 3 (RS): sl1 knitwise, k6, ssk, k1. Turn work.

Row 4 (WS): sl1 purlwise, p7, p2tog, p1. Turn work.

Continue decreasing in this way, increasing the number of sts in the centre by one on each row until all sts at the sides have been decreased. Then work one more WS row. **Note:** for the larger size, there will be no stitch left to k1/p1 at the end of the row after the last decrease.

Turn work. Divide heel sts evenly between two needles with 8 sts on each needle. Knit sts on RH needle. This point (centre back) is now the start of the round.

FOOT

Knit the 8 sts on LH needle from heel (needle I). Using a spare needle, pick up 14(15) sts from LH edge of heel flap + 1 st between heel flap and needle II. Knit picked up sts on to needle I, turning sts knitwise. Knit sts on needle II and needle III. Using the needle with 8 sts on it, pick up 14(15) sts from RH edge of heel flap + 1 st between heel flap and needle III. Knit picked up sts and 8 sts from heel on to needle IV, turning picked up sts knitwise. You now have 72(76) sts.

Continue in stocking (stockinette) stitch, decreasing for gusset as follows: k2tog at end of needle I and ssk at beginning of needle IV. Repeat decreases on every alt round until there are 13(14) sts left on each needle.

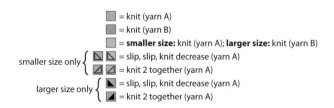

Chart I

Work rounds 1–89

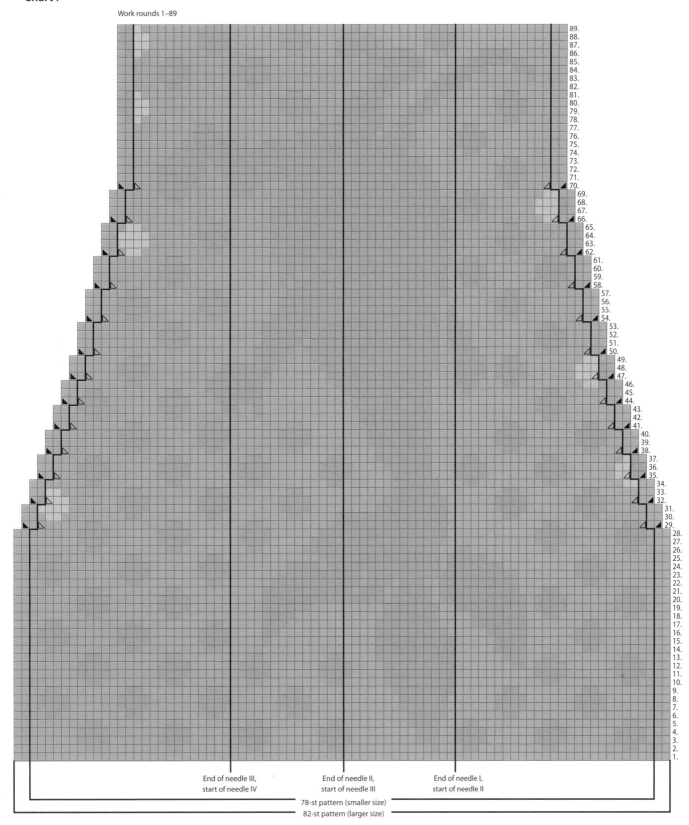

89.
88.
87.
86.
85.
84.
83.
82.
81.
80.
79.
78.
77.
76.
75.
74.
73.
72.
71.
70.
69.
68.
67.
66.
65.
64.
63.
62.
61.
60.
59.
58.
57.
56.
55.
54.
53.
52.
51.
50.
49.
48.
47.
46.
45.
44.
43.
42.
41.
40.
39.
38.
37.
36.
35.
34.
33.
32.
31.
30.
29.
28.
27.
26.
25.
24.
23.
22.
21.
20.
19.
18.
17.
16.
15.
14.
13.
12.
11.
10.
9.
8.
7.
6.
5.
4.
3.
2.
1.

End of needle III,
start of needle IV

End of needle II,
start of needle III

End of needle I,
start of needle II

78-st pattern (smaller size)

82-st pattern (larger size)

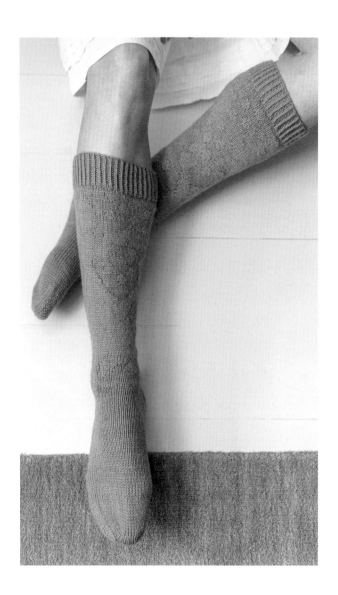

Continue in stocking (stockinette) stitch until the foot of the sock measures approximately 20.5(22)cm / 8(8¾)in or covers the wearer's little toe.

Start to decrease to work a wedge toe:

Needle I and needle III: work to last 3 sts, k2tog, k1.
Needle II and needle IV: k1, ssk, work to end.

Decrease as set on every alt round until there are 36 sts left and then work decreases on every round until there are 16 sts left.

Divide remaining sts evenly between two needles with 8 sts on the upper needle and 8 sts on the lower needle. Graft sts together. There are instructions and videos available online showing how to graft (sometimes called Kitchener stitch).

LEFT SOCK

Work as for right sock but work Fair Isle pattern for leg following Chart II.

FINISHING

Weave in ends. Carefully wet socks, place on a flat surface and block to measurements. Leave to dry. Steam block lightly if necessary.

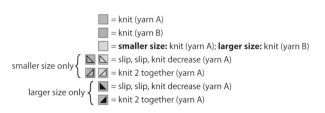

= knit (yarn A)
= knit (yarn B)
= **smaller size:** knit (yarn A); **larger size:** knit (yarn B)
smaller size only { = slip, slip, knit decrease (yarn A)
= knit 2 together (yarn A)
larger size only { = slip, slip, knit decrease (yarn A)
= knit 2 together (yarn A)

Chart II

Work rounds 1–89

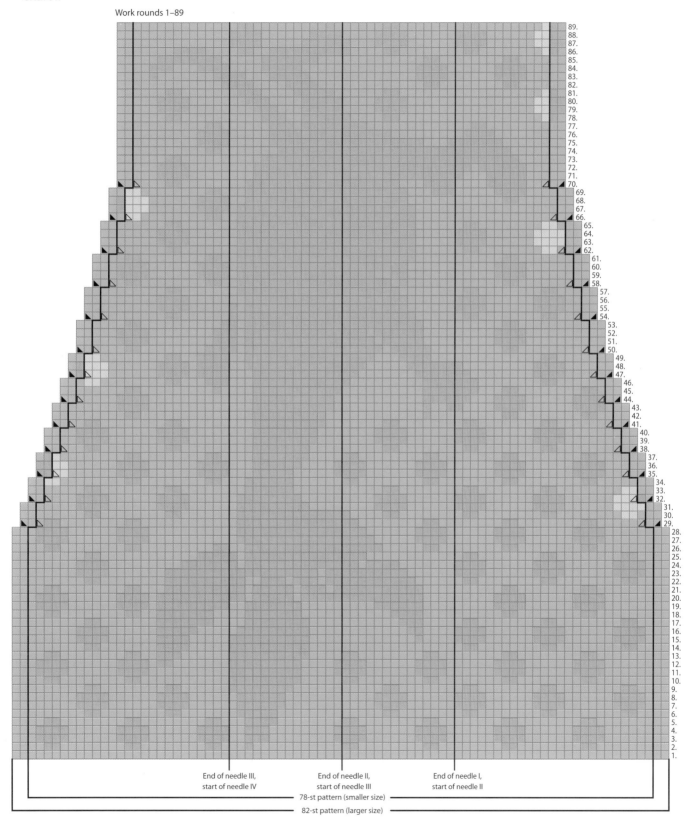

89.
88.
87.
86.
85.
84.
83.
82.
81.
80.
79.
78.
77.
76.
75.
74.
73.
72.
71.
70.
69.
68.
67.
66.
65.
64.
63.
62.
61.
60.
59.
58.
57.
56.
55.
54.
53.
52.
51.
50.
49.
48.
47.
46.
45.
44.
43.
42.
41.
40.
39.
38.
37.
36.
35.
34.
33.
32.
31.
30.
29.
28.
27.
26.
25.
24.
23.
22.
21.
20.
19.
18.
17.
16.
15.
14.
13.
12.
11.
10.
9.
8.
7.
6.
5.
4.
3.
2.
1.

End of needle III,
start of needle IV

End of needle II,
start of needle III

End of needle I,
start of needle II

78-st pattern (smaller size)

82-st pattern (larger size)

FLOWERS FOR SNORKMAIDEN

Snorkmaiden is having a relaxing afternoon picking flowers in a grassy field. The Fair Isle design of these two-colour socks is ideal for beginner knitters as the floats at the back of the work are short and the design has a simple repeat. A mosaic pattern decorates the feet of these socks, while diagonals make the soles more interesting.

DESIGNER Minttu Wikberg

SIZE UK 5/6 (Europe 38/39, US Women's 7½/8½, US Men's 6/7)

YARN

1 ball each of Novita Muumitalo (Moomin House) DK (8-ply/light worsted) yarn in Moomintroll 007 (A) and Snufkin 381 (B); 100g/3½oz/225m/246yd

AMOUNT USED

100g (3½oz) of yarns A and B

KNITTING NEEDLES

3mm (UK 11, US 2/3) double-pointed needles or size to obtain correct tension (gauge)

TECHNIQUES

Twisted rib in the round:
knit 1 through back loop, purl 1, repeat from * to *.

Stocking (stockinette) stitch in the round:
Knit all rounds.

Fair Isle in the round:
Work in stocking (stockinette) stitch following chart and instructions. Catch in any floats longer than 4 sts by twisting the yarns around each other at the back of the work. Vary where you catch your floats in the design so they don't land in the same place on consecutive rounds.

TENSION (GAUGE) 25 sts in st st = 10cm (4in)

NOTE

The socks are worked top down from cuff to toe.

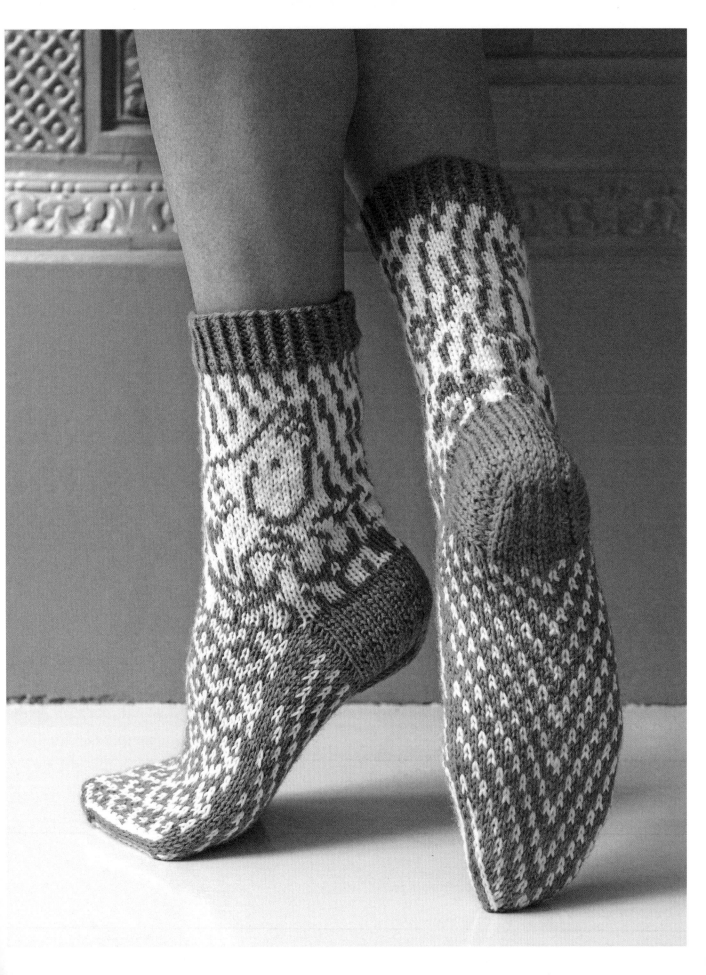

LEG

Cast on 56 sts in yarn B and divide equally between four needles with 14 sts on each needle. The start of the round is between needle I and needle IV at the back of the sock.

Join, being careful not to twist, and work 3cm (1¼in) in twisted rib in the round.

Start the Fair Isle pattern, working round 1 of Chart I A across all 56 sts. Then work rounds 2–42 of chart. Break off yarn A.

HEEL

Start to work heel by knitting the sts on needle I on to needle IV (28 sts for heel flap). Leave remaining sts on needles II and III. Turn work and start slip stitch pattern to reinforce heel:

Row 1 (WS): sl1 (with yarn at back of work), purl to end of row. Turn work.

Row 2 (RS): *sl1 (with yarn at back of work), k1*, repeat from * to * to end of row. Turn work.

Repeat rows 1 and 2 a total of 14 times and then knit 1 row (29 rows).

☐ = knit (yarn A)
▨ = knit (yarn B)

Chart I A

Work rounds 1–42

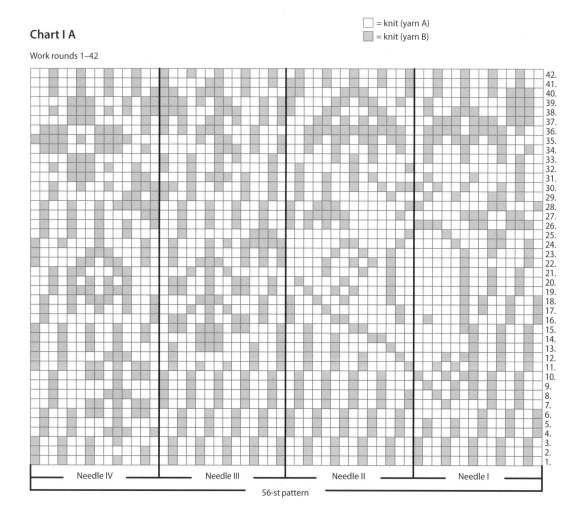

42.
41.
40.
39.
38.
37.
36.
35.
34.
33.
32.
31.
30.
29.
28.
27.
26.
25.
24.
23.
22.
21.
20.
19.
18.
17.
16.
15.
14.
13.
12.
11.
10.
9.
8.
7.
6.
5.
4.
3.
2.
1.

Needle IV   Needle III   Needle II   Needle I

56-st pattern

Start to decrease to turn the heel:

Continue in the same slip stitch pattern as before to reinforce heel. Starting with a RS row, work in pattern until there are 10 sts left on LH needle, skpo and turn work.

Sl1 purlwise and purl 8 sts on WS until there are 10 sts left on LH needle. P2tog and turn work.

Sl1 knitwise, work in pattern until there are 9 sts left on LH needle, skpo and turn work.

Continue as set working back and forth, i.e. always slip the first st of the row and skpo at the end of a RS row and p2tog at the end of a WS row. The number of sts at the sides will decrease by 1 each time, always leaving 10 sts in the centre. When you run out of side sts at the end of a WS row, k5 on RS.

This point (centre back) is now the start of the round.

FOOT

Knit 5 sts on LH needle from heel (needle I). Using a spare needle, pick up 14 sts from LH edge of heel flap + 1 st between heel flap and needle II. Knit picked up sts onto needle I, turning sts knitwise. Knit sts on needle II and needle III. Using the needle with 5 sts on it, pick up 14 sts from RH edge of heel flap + 1 st between heel flap and needle III. Knit picked up sts and 5 sts from heel on to needle IV, turning picked up sts knitwise. You now have 68 sts. Move 1 st from needle IV to needle III (for left sock move 1 st from needle I to needle II).

Chart I B

Work rounds 1–42

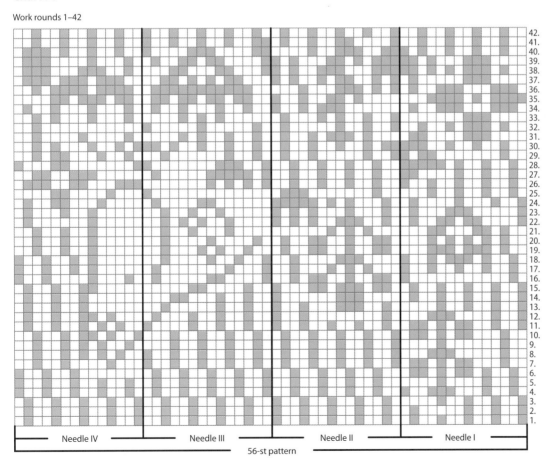

Needle IV	Needle III	Needle II	Needle I

56-st pattern

Continue in Fair Isle following Chart II A from round 2, starting to decrease for gusset at the same time as follows: k2tog at end of needle I and skpo at beginning of needle IV. Work these decreases on every alt round until there are 58 sts left. Work to the end of Chart II A.

Continue in Fair Isle repeating rounds 12–17 of Chart II A on needles I and IV and repeating rounds 10–17 on needles II and III. When foot measures approximately 19cm (7½in), start to decrease for the toe, continuing in Fair Isle pattern as set.

Decrease to work a wedge toe as follows:

Needle I and needle III: work in pattern to last 3 sts, k2tog, k1 in yarn B.

Needle II and needle IV: k1 in yarn B, k2tog through back loops in yarn A, work in pattern to end.

Decrease as set on every alt round until there are 38 sts left and then work decreases on every round until there are 18 sts left. **Note:** on the alt rounds with no decreases, work the toe decrease sts in the same yarn as on the previous round.

Finish by knitting 1 round in yarn B.

Graft the toe of the sock together or work a three-needle cast-/bind-off: transfer the last sts onto two safety pins and turn sock inside out. Transfer sts onto two needles, the upper sts on one and the lower sts on the other, and place them facing each other. *Knit the first stitch on each needle together*, repeat from * to * once. Slip the rightmost stitch on the RH needle over the leftmost stitch on the RH needle.

Knit the next pair of sts on the needles together and on the RH needle, lift the rightmost st over the leftmost st as when casting/binding off normally. Repeat from * to * to cast/bind off all sts.

SECOND SOCK

Work other sock as a mirror image following Charts I B and II B.

FINISHING

Weave in ends. Carefully wet socks, place on a flat surface and block to measurements. Leave to dry. Steam block lightly if necessary.

■ = knit (yarn B)
□ = knit (yarn A)
◤ = slip 1 stitch knitwise, knit 1 in yarn B
  and pass the slipped stitch over the knitted stitch
◣ = knit 2 together (yarn B)

Chart II A

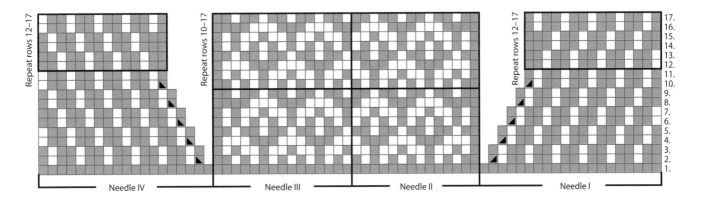

Chart II B

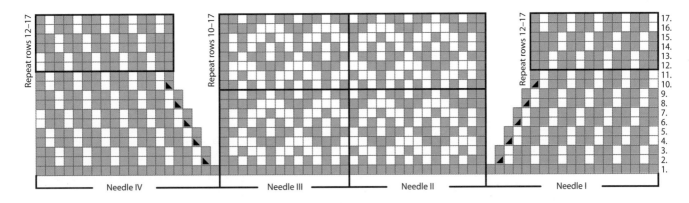

MYMBLE'S HERB GARDEN

Mymble finds the herb garden soothing in these leafy socks designed by Minttu Wikberg. A green creeper runs down the leg and the foot of these socks. There are two different sizes, for adults and children; the child's sock features only the creeper pattern, whereas Mymble is embroidered on to the adult's sock.

DESIGNER Minttu Wikberg

SIZES UK Child's 7(UK Adult's 5) (Europe 24(38), US Child's C8(US Women's 7½/US Men's 6))

YARN

1 ball each of Novita Muumitalo (Moomin House) DK (8-ply/light worsted) yarn in Moomintroll 007 (A), Snufkin 381 (B) and Snork 152 (C); 100g/3½oz/225m/246yd

For the larger size: Stinky 099 (D) and Fillyjonk 599 (E) for the embroidery.

AMOUNT USED

50(100)g / 1¾(3½)oz of yarns A and B and 25g (1oz) of yarn C for both sizes

KNITTING NEEDLES

3mm (UK 11, US 2/3) double-pointed needles or size to obtain correct tension (gauge)

TECHNIQUES

Twisted rib in the round:
knit 1 through back loop, purl 1, repeat from * to *.

Stocking (stockinette) stitch in the round:
Knit all rounds.

Fair Isle in the round:
Work in stocking (stockinette) stitch following chart and instructions. Catch in any floats longer than 4 sts by twisting the yarns around each other at the back of the work. Vary where you catch your floats in the design so they don't land in the same place on consecutive rounds.

TENSION (GAUGE) 25 sts in Fair Isle = 10cm (4in)

NOTE

The socks are worked bottom up from the toe to the cuff. For the larger size, Mymble is embroidered in duplicate stitch once the socks are finished. Use the ladder back jacquard technique to catch in the long floats in the panel where the Mymble design will go. You can find videos and instructions showing how to do this online.

RIGHT SOCK

Cast on 7(9) sts in yarn B. Working back and forth, purl 1 row and knit 1 row. Then use the yarn to pick up 7(9) sts from the cast-on edge (14(18) sts). Divide sts between four needles as shown for round 1 of Chart I(II A for larger size). Place different stitch markers at each side so you can tell which marks the start of the round. The start of the round is between needle I and needle IV at the side of the sock.

Work in stocking (stockinette) stitch in the round from round 2 of Chart I(II A), increasing at the same time: increase 1 st at beginning of needle I and needle III and increase 1 st at the end of needle II and needle IV at the stitch markers. Increase by lifting the strand of yarn between the sts on to the needle and knitting it through the back loop. **Note:** lift the strand of yarn between the sts on to the LH needle from the front at the beginning of needle I and needle III and from the back at the end of needle II and needle IV. Then work rounds 3–17(3–18) of chart. (Start the Fair Isle pattern from round 6(5) of chart and continue increasing as shown on chart.)

Continue in Fair Isle from round 1 of Chart III(IV A) and repeat rounds 1–6 until sock measures 12(19)cm / 4¾(7½)in from the toe.

Mark the position of the inserted heel: work the 11 + 10(14 + 14) sts on needles III and IV (for left foot on needles I and II) in a contrasting yarn. Break off contrasting yarn. Work sts in contrasting yarn on needles III and IV (for left foot sts on needles I and II) again now following chart. Continue working the 6 rounds of Chart III (the first 6 rounds of Chart IV A) and finish with round 6.

LEG

Child's size: continue in Fair Isle repeating rounds 1–6 of Chart III until the leg measures approximately 5cm (2in) from the contrasting yarn. Work chart to the end.

Adult's size: work rounds 7–59 of chart IV A. Work the Mymble section in yarn A (Mymble will be embroidered on in duplicate stitch once the sock is complete). In this yarn A panel, catch in the floats on the WS using the ladder back jacquard technique.

Both sizes: finally work 2(3)cm / ¾(1¼)in in twisted rib in yarn C. Cast/bind off in twisted rib.

HEEL

Carefully remove contrasting yarn and using yarn C, pick up 21(28) sts from above and below the hole and 2 additional sts from each side of the hole (46(60) sts). Place stitch markers at both edges, between the added sts. Divide sts evenly between four needles. The start of the round will be at the stitch marker at one side.

Work 1 round in stocking (stockinette) stitch in the round.

Start to decrease to turn heel:

Needle I and needle III: k1, k2tog through back loops, work to end.

Needle II and needle IV: work to last 3 sts, k2tog, k1.

Decrease as set on every alt round 3(4) more times and then on every round 4(5) times (14(20) sts).

Divide remaining sts evenly between two needles with 7(10) sts on the upper and lower needle. Graft sts together. There are instructions and videos available online showing how to graft (sometimes called Kitchener stitch).

Chart I

Work rounds 1–17

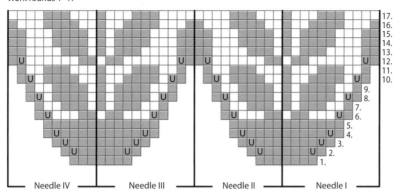

17.
16.
15.
14.
13.
12.
11.
10.
9.
8.
7.
6.
5.
4.
3.
2.
1.

Needle IV — Needle III — Needle II — Needle I

■ = knit (yarn B)

U = make 1 stitch by picking
up the yarn between the
stitches and knitting into
the back of it (yarn B)

□ = knit (yarn A)

Chart II A

Work rounds 1–18

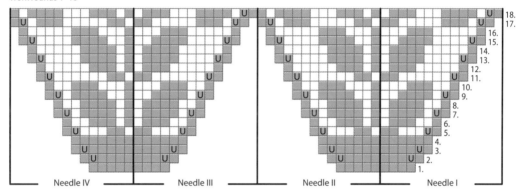

18.
17.
16.
15.
14.
13.
12.
11.
10.
9.
8.
7.
6.
5.
4.
3.
2.
1.

Needle IV — Needle III — Needle II — Needle I

Chart II B

Work rounds 1–18

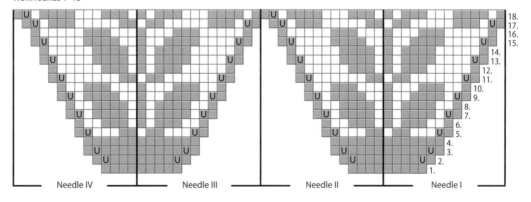

18.
17.
16.
15.
14.
13.
12.
11.
10.
9.
8.
7.
6.
5.
4.
3.
2.
1.

Needle IV — Needle III — Needle II — Needle I

Chart III

Repeat rounds 1–6

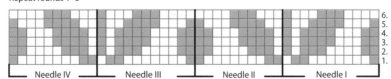

6.
5.
4.
3.
2.
1.

Needle IV — Needle III — Needle II — Needle I

Chart IV A

Repeat rounds 1–6

Needle IV   Needle III   Needle II   Needle I

LEFT SOCK

The child's sock is worked in the same way as the right sock.

The adult sock is worked as a mirror image using Charts II B and IV B.

FINISHING

For the adult sock, embroider the Mymble design in duplicate stitch following Charts IV A and IV B. Divide yarn D into two strands and embroider the facial features using short backstitches.

Weave in ends. Carefully wet socks, place on a flat surface and block to measurements. Leave to dry. Steam block lightly if necessary.

Chart IV B

59.
58.
57.
56.
55.
54.
53.
52.
51.
50.
49.
48.
47.
46.
45.
44.
43.
42.
41.
40.
39.
38.
37.
36.
35.
34.
33.
32.
31.
30.
29.
28.
27.
26.
25.
24.
23.
22.
21.
20.
19.
18.
17.
16.
15.
14.
13.
12.
11.
10.
9.
8.
7.
6.
5.
4.
3.
2.
1.

Repeat rounds 1–6

Needle IV ⎯ Needle III ⎯ Needle II ⎯ Needle I

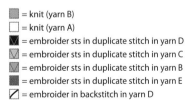

= knit (yarn B)
= knit (yarn A)
= embroider sts in duplicate stitch in yarn D
= embroider sts in duplicate stitch in yarn C
= embroider sts in duplicate stitch in yarn B
= embroider sts in duplicate stitch in yarn E
= embroider in backstitch in yarn D

ALL THAT GLITTERS

Sniff, with his long tail and pointy ears, inspired Sonja Nykänen to create these subtly coloured socks. The coins on the leg are worked in Fair Isle and the Sniff character is embroidered in duplicate stitch once the sock is complete.

DESIGNER Sonja Nykänen

SIZE UK 4/5 (Europe 37/38, US Women's 6½/7½, US Men's 5/6)

YARN

2 balls of Novita Muumitalo (Moomin House) DK (8-ply/light worsted) yarn in Ancestor 401 (A), 1 ball in Miffle 229 (B) and small amounts of Moomintroll 007 (C) and Stinky 099 (D) for the embroidery; 100g/3½oz/225m/246yd

Small amount of Novita Huviretki (Adventure) DK (8-ply/light worsted) in Beach 652 (E) for the embroidery; 50g/1¾oz/112m/122yd

AMOUNT USED

150g (5½oz) of yarn A and 50g (1¾oz) of yarn B

KNITTING NEEDLES

3mm (UK 11, US 2/3) double-pointed needles or size to obtain correct tension (gauge)

TECHNIQUES

K1, p1 rib in the round:
knit 1, purl 1, repeat from * to *.

K2, p2 rib in the round:
knit 2, purl 2, repeat from * to *.

Stocking (stockinette) stitch in the round:
Knit all rounds.

Fair Isle in the round:
Work in stocking (stockinette) stitch following chart and instructions. Catch in any floats longer than 3 sts by twisting the yarns around each other on the wrong side. Vary where you catch your floats in the design so they don't land in the same place on consecutive rounds.

TENSION (GAUGE) 24 sts in st st = 10cm (4in)

NOTE

The socks are worked top down from cuff to toe. Sniff and the numbers on the coins on the leg are embroidered on afterwards using duplicate stitch and backstitch. Divide yarn into two strands to sew the outline around Sniff.

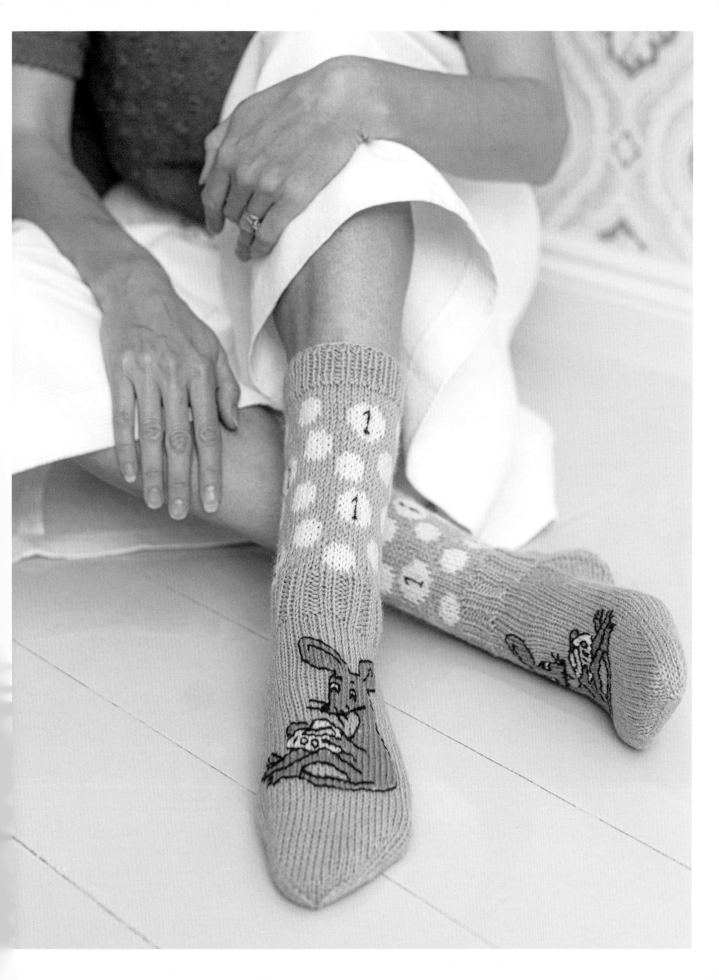

LEG

Cast/bind on 60 sts in yarn A and divide equally between four needles with 15 sts on each needle. The start of the round is between needle I and needle IV at the back of the sock.

Join, being careful not to twist, and work 3cm (1¼in) in k1, p1 rib in the round. Then knit 2 rounds.

Start the Fair Isle pattern following round 1 of Chart I and repeating the 30 st pattern twice. Then work rounds 2–16 of chart and repeat rounds 1–16.

Break off yarn B and work rest of sock in yarn A. Knit 1 round, decreasing 4 sts evenly across round (56 sts).

Work 3cm (1¼in) in k2, p2 rib. To make the rib look neater, you can divide the sts on your needles so that each needle holds an even number of sts. On last round of rib decrease 4 sts evenly across round (52 sts). Divide sts evenly with 13 sts on each needle.

HEEL

Start to work heel by knitting the sts on needle I on to needle IV (26 sts for heel flap). Leave remaining sts on needles II and III. Turn work. K2, p22, k2. Turn work and start slip stitch pattern with a garter stitch edge to reinforce heel:

Row 1 (RS): k2, *sl1 (with yarn at back of work), k1*, repeat from * to * until last 2 sts, k2. Turn work.

Row 2 (WS): k2, purl until last 2 sts, k2. Turn work.

Repeat rows 1 and 2 a total of 13 times (26 rows).

Start to decrease to turn the heel:

Continue in the same slip stitch pattern as before to reinforce heel. Starting with a RS row, work in pattern until there are 9 sts left on LH needle, skpo and turn work.

Then continue in slip stitch pattern but without the 2 sts in garter stitch at the edges:

Sl1 purlwise, purl 8 sts on WS until there are 9 sts left on LH needle, p2tog and turn work.

Chart I

Repeat rounds 1–16

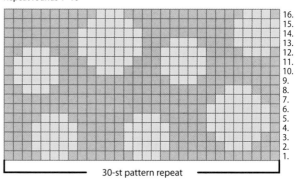

16.
15.
14.
13.
12.
11.
10.
9.
8.
7.
6.
5.
4.
3.
2.
1.

├──────── 30-st pattern repeat ────────┤

☐ = knit (yarn A)
☐ = knit (yarn B)

Starting with a RS row, sl1 knitwise, work in pattern until there are 8 sts left on LH needle, skpo and turn work.

Continue as set working back and forth, i.e. always slip the first st of the row and skpo at the end of a RS row and p2tog at the end of a WS row. The number of sts at the sides will decrease by 1 each time, always leaving 10 sts in the centre. When you run out of side sts at the end of a WS row, k5 on RS. This point (centre back) is now the start of the round.

FOOT

Knit 5 sts on LH needle from heel (needle I). Using a spare needle, pick up 13 sts from LH edge of heel flap + 1 st between heel flap and needle II. Knit picked up sts on to needle I, turning sts knitwise. Knit sts on needle II and needle III. Using the needle with 5 sts on it, pick up 13 sts from RH edge of heel flap + 1 st between heel flap and needle III. Knit picked up sts and 5 sts from heel on to needle IV, turning picked up sts knitwise. You now have 64 sts

Continue in stocking (stockinette) stitch, decreasing for gusset as follows: k2tog at end of needle I and skpo at beginning of needle IV.

Work this decrease on every alt round until there are 52 sts left.

Work in stocking (stockinette) stitch until the foot of the sock measures approximately 18cm (7in) or covers the wearer's little toe.

Now embroider Sniff in the centre front of the foot following Chart II A.

Continue in stocking (stockinette) stitch and start to decrease to work a barn toe:

Needle I and needle III: work to last 3 sts, k2tog, k1.

Needle II and needle IV: k1, skpo, work to end.

Decrease as set on every alt round until there are 28 sts left and then work decreases on every round until there are 8 sts left. Break yarn and thread through remaining sts.

SECOND SOCK

Work other sock in the same way but use Chart II B for the Sniff design.

FINISHING

Weave in ends. Carefully wet socks, place on a flat surface and block to measurements. Leave to dry. Steam block lightly if necessary.

⬛ = embroider sts in duplicate stitch in yarn E
⬜ = embroider sts in duplicate stitch in yarn B
⬜ = embroider sts in duplicate stitch in yarn C
◪ = embroider in backstitch in yarn D

Chart II A

37.
36.
35.
34.
33.
32.
31.
30.
29.
28.
27.
26.
25.
24.
23.
22.
21.
20.
19.
18.
17.
16.
15.
14.
13.
12.
11.
10.
9.
8.
7.
6.
5.
4.
3.
2.
1.

Chart II B

37.
36.
35.
34.
33.
32.
31.
30.
29.
28.
27.
26.
25.
24.
23.
22.
21.
20.
19.
18.
17.
16.
15.
14.
13.
12.
11.
10.
9.
8.
7.
6.
5.
4.
3.
2.
1.

THE HEMULEN'S GARDEN

Sonja Nykänen's gorgeous floral socks were inspired by the Hemulen's love of the natural world. A beautiful mock cable pattern at the ankle extends down to the heel and these lovely socks are finished off with a star toe.

DESIGNER Sonja Nykänen

SIZE UK 5/6 (Europe 38/39, US Women's 7½/8½, US Men's 6/7)

YARN
2 balls each of Novita Muumitalo (Moomin House) DK (8-ply/light worsted) yarn in Moomintroll 007 (A) and Hemulen 720 (B); 100g/3½oz/225m/246yd

AMOUNT USED
150g (5½oz) of yarns A and B

KNITTING NEEDLES
3mm (UK 11, US 2/3) double-pointed needles or size to obtain correct tension (gauge)

TECHNIQUES

Lace in the round:
Follow chart and instructions.

Stocking (stockinette) stitch in the round:
Knit all rounds.

Fair Isle in the round:
Work in stocking (stockinette) stitch following chart and instructions. Catch in any floats longer than 4 sts by twisting the yarns around each other at the back of the work. Vary where you catch your floats in the design so they don't land in the same place on consecutive rounds.

Mock cable in the round:
Follow chart and instructions.

TENSION (GAUGE) 25 sts in Fair Isle = 10cm (4in)

NOTE
The socks are worked top down from cuff to toe.

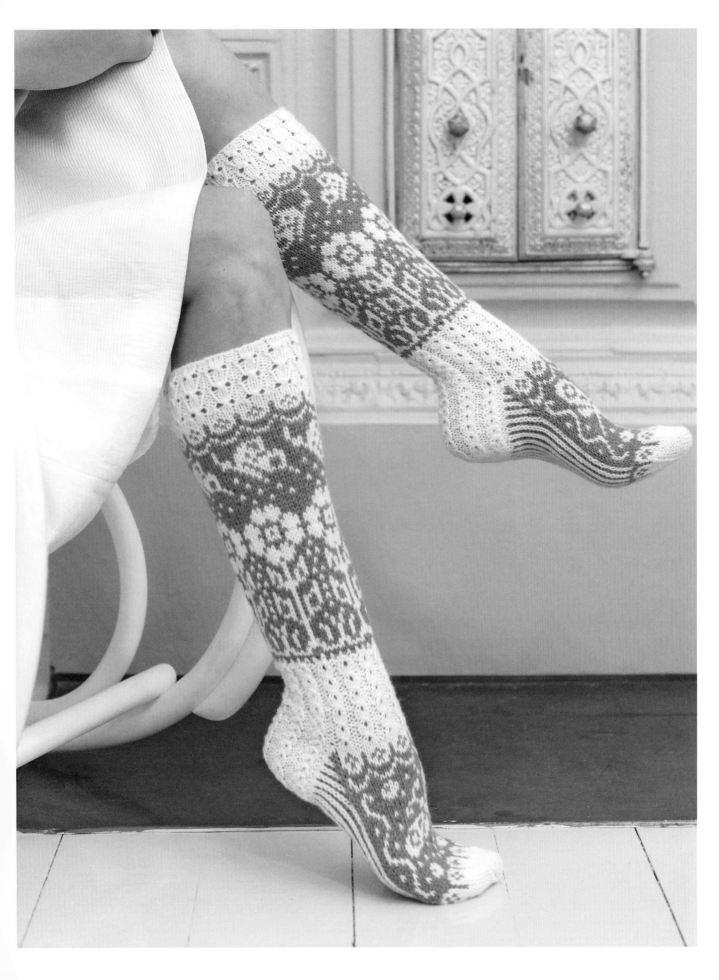

LEG

Cast on 70 sts in yarn A and divide between four needles as follows: 20 sts on needles I and III and 15 sts on needles II and IV. The start of the round is between needle I and needle IV at the back of the sock.

Join, being careful not to twist, and start working lace pattern in the round from round 1 of Chart I repeating the 5 st pattern 14 times. Work all 6 rounds of chart three times (18 rounds).

Chart I

Repeat rounds 1–6

5-st pattern repeat

□ = knit
− = purl
↑ = slip 1 stitch knitwise, knit 2 together and pass the slipped stitch over the knitted stitches

Then knit 2 rounds, increasing 2 sts evenly across first round (72 sts). Divide sts evenly with 18 sts on each needle.

Start the Fair Isle pattern, working round 1 of Chart II across all 72 sts. Then work rounds 2–60 of chart. Decrease at places marked on chart (64 sts).

Knit 1 round in yarn A, decreasing 4 sts evenly across round (60 sts). Divide sts evenly with 15 sts on each needle.

Start working mock cable pattern in the round in yarn A from round 1 of Chart III repeating the 5-st pattern 12 times. Work all 4 rounds of the chart five times and then work rounds 1–3 again (23 rounds).

Chart III

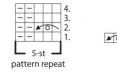

5-st pattern repeat

□ = knit on RS and purl on WS
− = purl on RS and knit on WS
= slip 3 stitches on to right-hand needle, pass the rightmost stitch over the other 2 stitches, slip the other 2 stitches back on to the left-hand needle and knit 1, yarn over, knit 1

HEEL

Move the last st on needle I to needle II and the last st on needle III to needle IV. Start to work heel by knitting the sts on needle I on to needle IV, knitting knit sts and purling purl sts (the row will end with one purl st) (30 sts for heel flap). Leave remaining sts on needles II and III. Turn work and continue knitting knit sts and purling purl sts; work 1 row.

Continue working mock cable pattern back and forth following Chart IV: start row 1 from the right-hand side of the chart (RS), repeat the 5-st pattern five times and k1 at left-hand side. Work all 4 rows of chart six times and then work rows 1 and 2 again (26 rows).

Chart IV

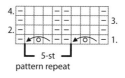

5-st pattern repeat

Start to work in stocking (stockinette) stitch to turn a French (rounded) heel:

Row 1 (RS): sl1 (with yarn at back of work), k16, skpo, k1. Turn work.

Row 2 (WS): sl1 purlwise, p5, p2tog, p1. Turn work.

Row 3: sl1 knitwise, k6, skpo, k1. Turn work.

Row 4: sl1 purlwise, p7, p2tog, p1. Turn work.

Row 5: sl1 knitwise, k8, skpo, k1. Turn work.

Continue decreasing in this way, increasing the number of sts in the centre by one on each row until the last st on both the RS and WS is right at the edge of the heel flap and you have 18 sts left. The last row will be a WS row.

Divide heel sts evenly between two needles with 9 sts on each needle. Knit sts on RH needle. This point (centre back) is now the start of the round. Divide sts on needles II and III evenly with 15 sts on each needle.

Chart II

Work rounds 1–60

= knit (yarn B)

= knit (yarn A)

= slip 1 stitch knitwise, knit 1 in yarn B and pass the slipped stitch over the knitted stitch

= knit 2 together (yarn B)

= slip 1 stitch knitwise, knit 1 in yarn A and pass the slipped stitch over the knitted stitch

= knit 2 together (yarn A)

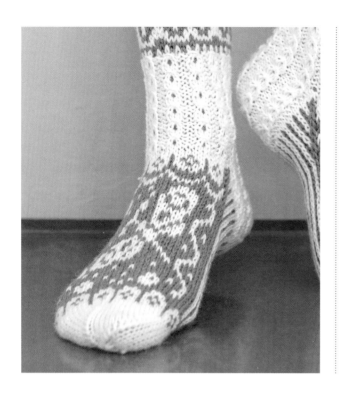

FOOT

Knit the 9 sts on LH needle from heel (needle I). Using a spare needle, pick up 14 sts from LH edge of heel flap + 1 st between heel flap and needle II. Knit picked up sts on to needle I, turning sts knitwise. Knit sts on needle II and needle III. Using the needle with 9 sts on it, pick up 14 sts from RH edge of heel flap + 1 st between heel flap and needle III. Knit picked up sts and 9 sts from heel on to needle IV, turning picked up sts knitwise. You now have 78 sts and have worked the first round of Chart V A.

Work rounds 2–42 of Chart V A. Work gusset decreases as shown in chart: k2tog at end of needle I and skpo at beginning of needle IV. Work decreases on every round until there are 60 sts left. Then continue working to the end of Chart V A.

Chart V A

Work rounds 1–42

Break off yarn B. If necessary work additional rounds in stocking (stockinette) stitch in yarn A, until the foot of the sock fully covers the wearer's little toe (this sock has a short toe).

Continue in stocking (stockinette) stitch and start to work the star toe: at the end of each needle, k2tog through back loops. Repeat these decreases on every round until there are 8 sts left. Break off yarn and thread through remaining stitches.

SECOND SOCK

Work other sock in the same way but following Chart V B for the foot.

FINISHING

Weave in ends. Carefully wet socks, place on a flat surface and block to measurements. Leave to dry. Steam block lightly if necessary.

■ = knit (yarn B)
☐ = knit (yarn A)
◣ = slip 1 stitch knitwise, knit 1 in yarn B and pass the slipped stitch over the knitted stitch
◢ = knit 2 together (yarn B)

Chart V B

Work rounds 1–42

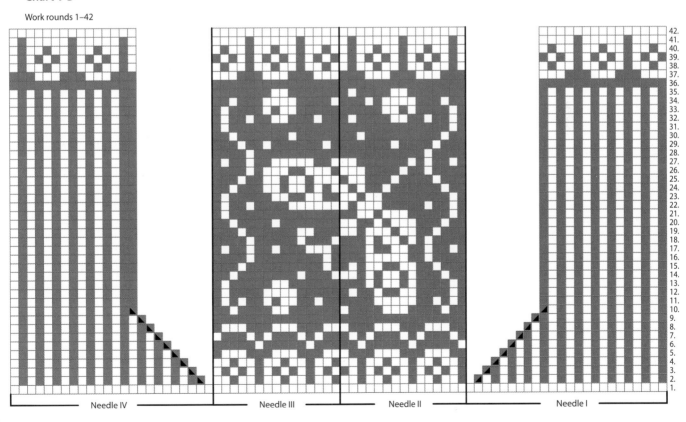

Needle IV   Needle III   Needle II   Needle I

AN INDEPENDENT THINKER

Kind Too-Ticky is standing by the jetty in these socks designed by Minttu Wikberg. A bright palette of colours and rapidly changing designs make this an interesting pattern to knit. The Fair Isle pattern with its changing colours is easy to knit as the floats are short. There are separate versions of this sock for adults and children.

DESIGNER Minttu Wikberg

SIZES UK Child's 7(UK Adult's 5) (Europe 24(38), US child's size 7(US Women's 7½, US Men's 6))

YARN

1 ball each of Novita Muumitalo (Moomin House) DK (8-ply/light worsted) yarn in Moomintroll 007 (A), Fillyjonk 599 (B), Snork 152 (C), Miffle 229 (D) and Stinky 099 (E); 100g/3½oz/225m/246yd

For the larger size, you will need small amounts of Snorkmaiden 507 (F) or other pink yarn for the embroidery.

AMOUNT USED

50g/1¾oz (100g/3½oz) of yarn A, 25g/1oz (50g /1¾oz) of yarn B, a small amount/25g (1oz) of yarns C and E and 50g (1¾oz) of yarn D

KNITTING NEEDLES

3mm (UK 11, US 2/3) double-pointed needles or size to obtain correct tension (gauge)

TECHNIQUES

Twisted rib in the round:
knit 1 through back loop, purl 1, repeat from * to *.

Stocking (stockinette) stitch in the round:
Knit all rounds.

Fair Isle in the round:
Work in stocking (stockinette) stitch following chart and instructions. Catch in any floats longer than 4 sts by twisting the yarns around each other at the back of the work. Vary where you catch your floats in the design so they don't land in the same place on consecutive rounds.

TENSION (GAUGE) 25 sts in Fair Isle = 10cm (4in)

NOTE

The socks are worked top down from cuff to toe. The heel is inserted at the end. In the adult size, Too-Ticky's face and part of her hat and trousers are embroidered at the end following the instructions.

LEG

Cast on 42(68) sts in yarn A and divide between four needles as follows: needle I 11(20) sts, needle II 10(14) sts, needle III 10(14) sts and needle IV 11(20) sts. The start of the round is between needle I and needle IV at the back of the sock.

Join, being careful not to twist, and work 2(3)cm / ¾(1¼)in in twisted rib in the round. Then knit one round in yarn A.

Start the Fair Isle pattern following round 1 of Chart I(II A for the larger size). Continue as follows:

Child's size: continue in Fair Isle from round 2 of chart onwards until the leg measures approximately 8cm (3¼in) or desired length.

Adult's size: work rounds 2–52 of chart. Decrease at places marked on chart. **Note:** embroider the stitches on rounds 8 and 9 in yarn C, Too-Ticky's facial features, and the stitches on rounds 42 and 43 in yarn E on to the finished sock at the end. While knitting the sock, work these stitches in yarn A.

Both sizes: on the next round, mark the position of the inserted heel. Work sts on needles I–III as shown for next round on chart. Work sts on needle IV and needle I in a contrasting yarn. Break off contrasting yarn. Work sts on needle IV again, working to end of round following chart (42(56) sts).

Chart I

= knit (yarn C)

= knit (yarn A)

= knit (yarn D)

= knit (yarn B)

= knit (yarn E)

= knit 2 together through back loops (yarn A)

= knit 2 together (yarn A)

= knit 2 together through back loops (yarn B)

= knit 2 together (yarn B)

= knit 2 together through back loops (yarn E)

= knit 2 together (yarn E)

= embroider sts in duplicate stitch in yarn C/yarn E

= backstitch in yarn E

= satin stitch in yarn C/yarn F

= French knot in yarn E

Chart II A

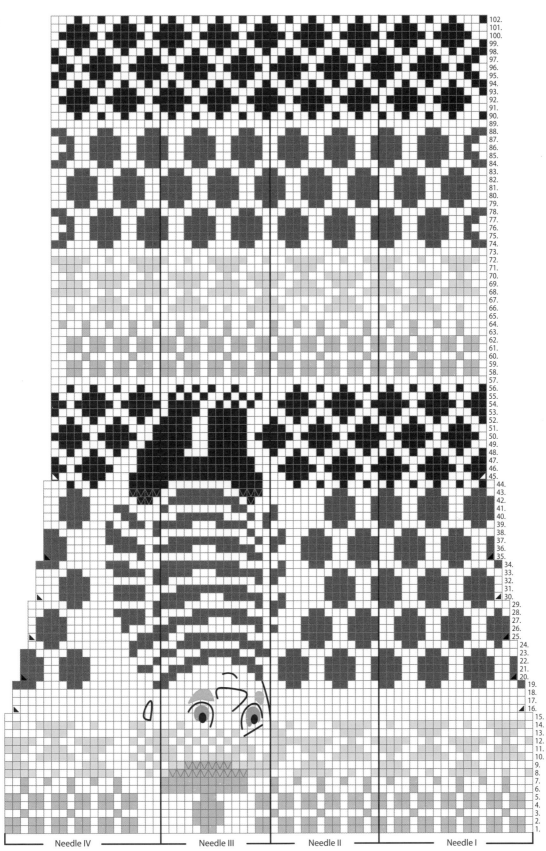

102.
101.
100.
99.
98.
97.
96.
95.
94.
93.
92.
91.
90.
89.
88.
87.
86.
85.
84.
83.
82.
81.
80.
79.
78.
77.
76.
75.
74.
73.
72.
71.
70.
69.
68.
67.
66.
65.
64.
63.
62.
61.
60.
59.
58.
57.
56.
55.
54.
53.
52.
51.
50.
49.
48.
47.
46.
45.
44.
43.
42.
41.
40.
39.
38.
37.
36.
35.
34.
33.
32.
31.
30.
29.
28.
27.
26.
25.
24.
23.
22.
21.
20.
19.
18.
17.
16.
15.
14.
13.
12.
11.
10.
9.
8.
7.
6.
5.
4.
3.
2.
1.

Needle IV · Needle III · Needle II · Needle I

63

FOOT

Continue in Fair Isle following chart, starting by working on top of the sts in contrasting yarn on needle I, until foot measures 8(14)cm / 3¼(5½)in from the contrasting yarn to mark the heel. You do not necessarily have to work the chart to the end. If you need your sock to be longer, start repeating the chart from the start for the child's size or from round 57 for the adult's size.

Then knit 1 round in yarn A. Finish sock in yarn B, starting to decrease for the toe at the same time. **Note:** if you are in the middle of a motif, complete it as you work the toe decreases, then knit 1 round in yarn A and finish your toe in yarn B. For the child's sock, decrease 1 st on needles I and IV on the first round of the red section so that you have the same number of sts on all needles.

Work a barn toe as follows:

Needle I and needle III: work to last 3 sts, k2tog, k1.

Needle II and needle IV: k1, skpo, work to end.

Decrease as set on every alt round until there are 24 sts left and then work decreases on every round until there are 8 sts left. Break yarn and thread through remaining sts.

HEEL

Carefully remove contrasting yarn and using yarn C, pick up 22(28) sts from above and below the hole and 2 additional sts from each side of the hole (48(60) sts). Place stitch markers at both edges, between the added sts. Divide sts evenly between four needles. The start of the round will be at the stitch marker at one side.

Work 1 round in stocking (stockinette) stitch in the round.

Start to decrease to turn heel:

Needle I and needle III: k1, k2tog through back loops, work to end.

Needle II and needle IV: work to last 3 sts, k2tog, k1.

Decrease as set on every alt round 3(4) more times and then on every round 4(5) times (16(20) sts).

Divide remaining sts evenly between two needles with 8(10) sts for the heel on the upper and lower needle. Graft sts together. There are instructions and videos available online showing how to graft (sometimes called Kitchener stitch).

SECOND SOCK

Work other sock in the same way for the child's version but use chart II B to reverse the design for the adult's version.

FINISHING

Adult's size: embroider the main facial features (eye shape, face shape, nose, mouth and ear) using short backstitches and yarn E with yarn divided into two strands. Embroider the eye in yarn C and the pink cheeks in yarn F using satin stitch. Work French knots in yarn E for the pupils. Embroider the missing stitches on rounds 8, 9, 42 and 43 in duplicate stitch.

Weave in ends. Carefully wet socks, place on a flat surface and block to measurements. Leave to dry. Steam block lightly if necessary.

▢	= knit (yarn C)
▢	= knit (yarn A)
▢	= knit (yarn D)
▢	= knit (yarn B)
■	= knit (yarn E)
◪	= knit 2 together through back loops (yarn A)
◩	= knit 2 together (yarn A)
◪	= knit 2 together through back loops (yarn B)
◩	= knit 2 together (yarn B)
◪	= knit 2 together through back loops (yarn E)
◩	= knit 2 together (yarn E)
▽ ▼	= embroider sts in duplicate stitch in yarn C/yarn E
◿	= backstitch in yarn E
◺ ◺	= satin stitch in yarn C/yarn F
◉	= French knot in yarn E

Chart II B

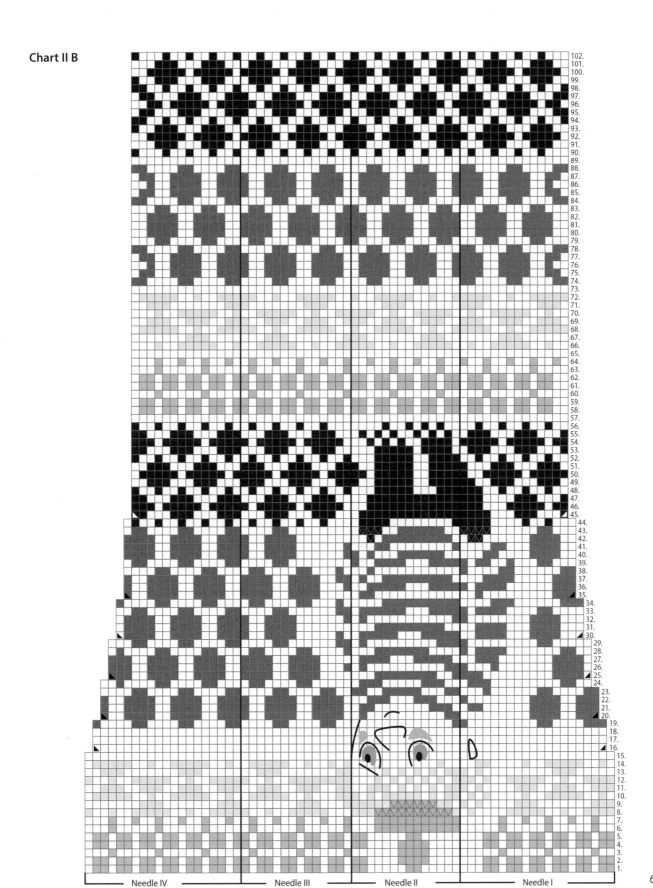

102.
101.
100.
99.
98.
97.
96.
95.
94.
93.
92.
91.
90.
89.
88.
87.
86.
85.
84.
83.
82.
81.
80.
79.
78.
77.
76.
75.
74.
73.
72.
71.
70.
69.
68.
67.
66.
65.
64.
63.
62.
61.
60.
59.
58.
57.
56.
55.
54.
53.
52.
51.
50.
49.
48.
47.
46.
45.
44.
43.
42.
41.
40.
39.
38.
37.
36.
35.
34.
33.
32.
31.
30.
29.
28.
27.
26.
25.
24.
23.
22.
21.
20.
19.
18.
17.
16.
15.
14.
13.
12.
11.
10.
9.
8.
7.
6.
5.
4.
3.
2.
1.

Needle IV. ————— Needle III ————— Needle II ————— Needle I

CHRISTMAS IS COMING

These impressive long socks are so Christmassy. Beneath the cable cuffs, the Moomins are decorating the tree. The mock cable pattern at the ankle extends down the heel. Hearts decorate the foot, partnered with a cheerful stripe pattern on the soles.

DESIGNER Sonja Nykänen

SIZE UK 5/6 (Europe 38/39, US Women's 7½/8½, US Men's 6/7)

YARN

2 balls each of Novita Muumitalo (Moomin House) DK (8-ply/light worsted) yarn in Moomintroll 007 (A) and Fillyjonk 599 (B); 100g/3½oz/225m/246yd

AMOUNT USED

150g (5½oz) of yarns A and B

KNITTING NEEDLES

3mm (UK 11, US 2/3) double-pointed needles or size to obtain correct tension (gauge)

Cable needle

TECHNIQUES

Cable in the round:
Follow chart and instructions.

Stocking (stockinette) stitch in the round:
Knit all rounds.

Fair Isle in the round:
Work in stocking (stockinette) stitch following chart and instructions. Catch in any floats longer than 4 sts by twisting the yarns around each other at the back of the work. Vary where you catch your floats in the design so they don't land in the same place on consecutive rounds.

Mock cable in the round and worked flat:
Follow chart and instructions.

TENSION (GAUGE) 25 sts in Fair Isle = 10cm (4in)

NOTE

The socks are worked top down from cuff to toe. The Moomins' facial features are embroidered following the instructions once the socks are finished.

LEG

Cast on 72 sts in yarn A and divide evenly between four needles with 18 sts on each needle. The start of the round is between needle I and needle IV at the back of the sock.

Join, being careful not to twist, and start working cable pattern in the round starting at round 1 of Chart I and repeating the 6-st pattern 12 times. Then work rounds 2–16 of chart.

Start the Fair Isle pattern, working round 1 of Chart II across all 72 sts. Work rounds 2–68 of chart. Decrease at places marked on chart: at end of round, skpo and k2tog at start of next round so that the decreases appear at the same height at the back of the sock. **Note:** on round 52, divide sts between needles as follows: needle I 18 sts, needle II 15 sts, needle III 15 sts and needle IV 18 sts.

At the end of Chart II you will have 60 sts.

Start working mock cable pattern in the round in yarn A from round 1 of Chart III repeating the 5-st pattern 12 times. Work all 4 rounds of chart five times and then work rounds 1–3 of chart (23 rounds).

HEEL

Move the last st on needle I to needle II and the last st on needle III to needle IV. Start to work heel by knitting the sts on needle I on to needle IV, knitting knit sts and purling purl sts (the row will end with one purl st) (30 sts for heel flap). Leave remaining sts on needles II and III. Turn work and continue knitting knit sts and purling purl sts; work one row.

Continue working mock cable pattern back and forth following Chart IV: start row 1 from the right-hand side of the chart (RS), repeat the 5-st pattern five times and k1 at left-hand side. Work all 4 rows of chart six times and then work rows 1 and 2 of chart (26 rows).

Start to work in stocking (stockinette) stitch to turn a French (rounded) heel:

Row 1 (RS): sl1 (with yarn at back of work), k16, skpo, k1. Turn work.

Row 2 (WS): sl1 purlwise, p5, p2tog, p1. Turn work.

Row 3: sl1 knitwise, k6, skpo, k1. Turn work.

Row 4: sl1 purlwise, p7, p2tog, p1. Turn work.

Row 5: sl1 knitwise, k8, skpo, k1. Turn work.

Chart I

Work rounds 1–16

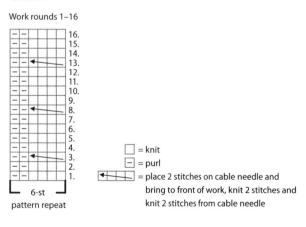

= knit

= purl

= place 2 stitches on cable needle and bring to front of work, knit 2 stitches and knit 2 stitches from cable needle

6-st pattern repeat

Chart III

5-st pattern repeat

Chart IV

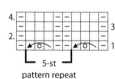

5-st pattern repeat

= knit on RS and purl on WS

= purl on RS and knit on WS

= slip 3 stitches on to right-hand needle, pass the rightmost stitch over the other 2 stitches, slip the other 2 stitches back on to the left-hand needle and knit 1, yarn over, knit 1

Chart II

Work rounds 1–68

Needle IV   Needle III   Needle II   Needle I

72-st pattern

□ = knit (yarn A)
■ = knit (yarn B)
◣ = slip 1 stitch knitwise, knit 1 in yarn B and pass the slipped stitch over the knitted stitch
◪ = knit 2 together (yarn B)
◩ = slip 1 stitch knitwise, knit 1 yarn A and pass the slipped stitch over the knitted stitch
◪ = embroider in backstitch in yarn B

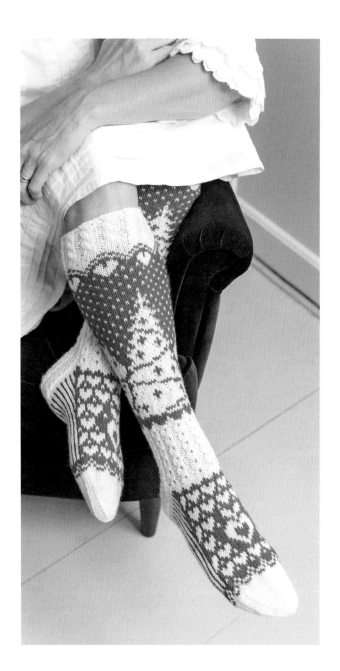

Continue decreasing in this way, increasing the number of sts in the centre by one on each row until the last st on both the RS and WS is right at the edge of the heel flap and you have 18 sts left. The last row will be a WS row.

Divide heel sts evenly between two needles with 9 sts on each needle. Knit sts on RH needle. This point (centre back) is now the start of the round. Divide sts on needles II and III evenly with 15 sts on each needle.

FOOT

Knit the 9 sts on LH needle from heel (needle I). Using a spare needle, pick up 14 sts from LH edge of heel flap + 1 st between heel flap and needle II. Knit picked up sts on to needle I, turning sts knitwise. Knit sts on needle II and needle III. Using the needle with 9 sts on it, pick up 14 sts from RH edge of heel flap + 1 st between heel flap and needle III. Knit picked up sts and 9 sts from heel on to needle IV, turning picked up sts knitwise. You now have 78 sts and have worked the first round of Chart V.

Work rounds 2–39 of Chart V. Work gusset decreases as shown on chart: k2tog at end of needle I and skpo at beginning of needle IV. Repeat decreases on every alt round until there are 60 sts left. Then continue working to the end of Chart V.

Break off yarn B. If necessary, work additional rounds in stocking (stockinette) stitch in yarn A until the foot of the sock fully covers the wearer's little toe.

Continue in stocking (stockinette) stitch and start to work barn toe:

Needle I and needle III: work to last 3 sts, k2tog, k1.

Needle II and needle IV: k1, skpo, work to end.

Decrease as set on every alt round until there are 32 sts left and then work decreases on every round until there are 8 sts left. Break yarn and thread through remaining sts.

SECOND SOCK
Work the other sock in the same way.

FINISHING
Weave in ends. Embroider the details on Moomintroll and Snorkmaiden as shown on Chart II in backstitch using yarn B, dividing the yarn into two strands. Make a French knot for the pupils. Work the same embroidery on the second sock or embroider Moomintroll and Snorkmaiden on opposite sides.

Carefully wet socks, place on a flat surface and block to measurements. Leave to dry. Steam block lightly if necessary.

Chart V

Work rounds 1–39

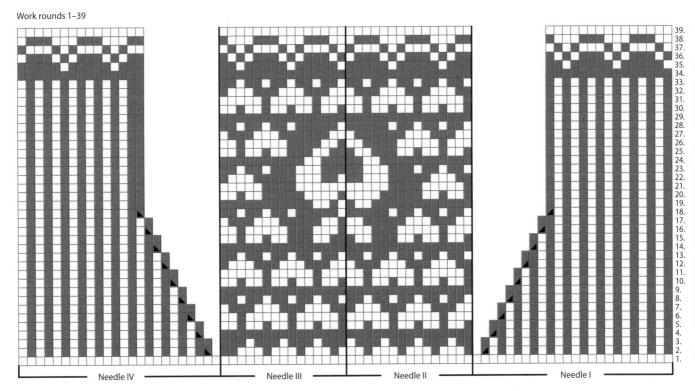

Needle IV   Needle III   Needle II   Needle I

 = knit (yarn A)
▨ = knit (yarn B)
◣ = slip 1 stitch knitwise, knit 1 in yarn B and pass the slipped stitch over the knitted stitch
◢ = knit 2 together (yarn B)

DIVING FOR PEARLS

Moomintroll has dived into a lake edged with reeds in these socks designed by Sonja Nykänen. The socks have a ribbed cuff, a reinforced heel and a barn toe. The leg of the sock is worked in Fair Isle while Moomintroll himself is added in duplicate stitch once the socks are complete.

DESIGNER Sonja Nykänen

SIZE UK 2½/3½ (Europe 35/36, US Women's 5/6, US Men's 3½/4)

YARN
1 ball each of Novita Muumitalo (Moomin House) DK (8-ply/light worsted) yarn in Moomintroll 007 (A), Snork 152 (B), Miffle 229 (C), Snufkin 381 (D) and a small amount of Stinky 099 (E); 100g/3½oz/225m/246yd

AMOUNT USED
50g (1¾oz) of yarn A, 100g (3½oz) of yarn B and 25g (1oz) of yarns C and D

KNITTING NEEDLES
3mm (UK 11, US 2/3) double-pointed needles or size to obtain correct tension (gauge)

TECHNIQUES

Rib in the round:
knit 1, purl 1, repeat from * to *.

Stocking (stockinette) stitch in the round:
Knit all rounds.

Fair Isle in the round:
Work in stocking (stockinette) stitch following chart and instructions. Catch in any floats longer than 3 sts by twisting the yarns around each other on the wrong side. Vary where you catch your floats in the design so they don't land in the same place on consecutive rounds.

TENSION (GAUGE) 24 sts in st st = 10cm (4in)

NOTE
The socks are worked top down from cuff to toe. Embroider Moomintroll and the reeds in the water on at the end using duplicate stitch, satin stitch and backstitch. Divide yarn E into two strands to sew the outline around Moomintroll.

LEFT SOCK

Cast on 52 sts in yarn A and divide evenly between four needles with 13 sts on each needle. The start of the round is between needle I and needle IV at the back of the sock.

Join, being careful not to twist, and work 3cm (1¼in) in rib in the round. Then knit 1 round.

Start the Fair Isle pattern following round 1 of Chart I and repeating the 4-st pattern 13 times. Then work round 2 of chart.

Work in stocking (stockinette) stitch in stripes as follows: *knit 3 rounds in yarn C, knit 3 rounds in yarn A*, repeat from * to *, knit 4 rounds in yarn B, knit 3 rounds in yarn A, knit 3 rounds in yarn C, knit 4 rounds in yarn A.

Now start Fair Isle pattern from round 1 of Chart II, repeating the 4-st pattern 13 times. Then work rounds 2–10 of chart. Work 2 rounds in yarn B and break off other yarns. Work the rest of the sock in yarn B.

Chart I

Work rounds 1 and 2

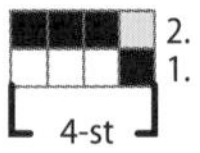

4-st
pattern repeat

= knit (yarn A)
= knit (yarn E)
= knit (yarn C)

Chart II

Work rounds 1–10

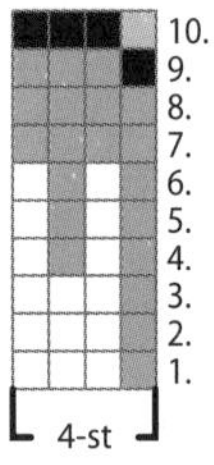

4-st
pattern repeat

= knit (yarn A)
= knit (yarn D)
= knit (yarn E)
= knit (yarn B)

HEEL

Start to work heel by knitting the sts on needle I on to needle IV (26 sts for heel flap). Leave remaining sts on needles II and III. Turn work. K2, p22, k2. Turn work and start slip stitch pattern with a garter stitch edge to reinforce heel:

Row 1 (RS): k2, *sl1 (with yarn at back of work), k1*, repeat from * to * until last 2 sts, k2. Turn work.

Row 2 (WS): k2, purl until last 2 sts, k2. Turn work.

Repeat rows 1 and 2 a total of 13 times (26 rows).

Start to decrease to turn the heel:

Continue in the same slip stitch pattern as before to reinforce heel. Starting with a RS row, work in pattern until there are 9 sts left on LH needle, skpo and turn work.

Then continue in slip stitch pattern but without the 2 sts in garter stitch at the edges:

WS row: sl1 purlwise, purl 8 sts on WS until there are 9 sts left on LH needle, p2tog and turn work.

RS row: sl1 knitwise, work in pattern until there are 8 sts left on LH needle, skpo and turn work.

Continue as set working back and forth, i.e. always slip the first st of the row and skpo at the end of a RS row and p2tog at the end of a WS row. The number of sts at the sides will decrease by 1 each time, always leaving 10 sts in the centre. When you run out of side sts at the end of a WS row, k5 on RS. This point is now the start of the round.

FOOT

Knit 5 sts on LH needle from heel (needle I). Using a spare needle, pick up 13 sts from LH edge of heel flap + 1 st between heel flap and needle II. Knit picked up sts on to needle I, turning sts knitwise. Knit sts on needle II and needle III. Using the needle with 5 sts on it, pick up 13 sts from RH edge of heel flap + 1 st between heel flap and needle III. Knit picked up sts and 5 sts from heel on to needle IV, turning picked up sts knitwise. You now have 64 sts.

Continue in stocking (stockinette) stitch, decreasing for gusset as follows: k2tog at end of needle I and skpo at beginning of needle IV. Work this decrease on every alt round until there are 52 sts left.

Work in stocking (stockinette) stitch until the foot of the sock measures approximately 18cm (7in) or covers the wearer's little toe.

Continue in stocking (stockinette) stitch and start to decrease for barn toe:

Needle I and needle III: work to last 3 sts, k2tog, k1.

Needle II and needle IV: k1, skpo, work to end.

Decrease as set on every alt round until there are 28 sts left.

Now embroider Moomintroll from Chart III A on to the sock so that the lowest reed in the water is in the middle of the sock close to the toe.

Then repeat the toe decreases on every round until there are 8 sts left. Break off yarn and thread through remaining stitches.

RIGHT SOCK

Work in the same way as the left sock but use Chart III B for the embroidery on the foot.

FINISHING

Weave in ends. Carefully wet socks, place on a flat surface and block to measurements. Leave to dry. Steam block lightly if necessary.

Chart III A

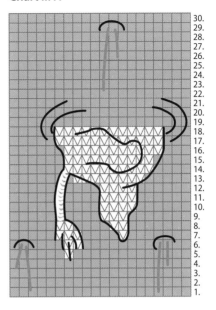

Chart III B

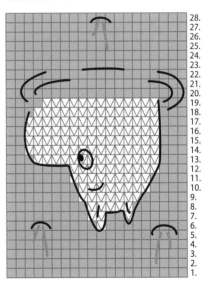

☐ = embroider sts in duplicate stitch in yarn A

◨ = embroider sts on top in satin stitch in yarn A

◩ = embroider in backstitch in yarn E

◪ = embroider simple long stitches sts in yarn D

THE WANDERER

Snufkin is often in a travelling mood, even after dark. These stylish black and white socks are roomy and fit men's feet. They have a traditional ribbed cuff, a reinforced heel and a star toe.

DESIGNER Minttu Wikberg
SIZE UK 9½ (Europe 44, US Women's 12, US Men's 10½)
YARN
1 ball of Novita Muumitalo (Moomin House) DK (8-ply/light worsted) yarn in Moomintroll, 007 (A) and 2 balls in Stinky 099 (B); 100g/3½oz/225m/246yd
AMOUNT USED
50g (1¾oz) of yarn A and 150g (5½oz) of yarn B
KNITTING NEEDLES
3mm (UK 11, US 2/3) double-pointed needles or size to obtain correct tension (gauge)

TECHNIQUES
Rib in the round:
knit 1, purl 1, repeat from * to *.
Stocking (stockinette) stitch in the round:
Knit all rounds.
Fair Isle in the round:
Work in stocking (stockinette) stitch following chart and instructions. Catch in any floats longer than 4 sts by twisting the yarns around each other at the back of the work. Vary where you catch your floats in the design so they don't land in the same place on consecutive rounds.
TENSION (GAUGE) 25 sts in st st = 10cm (4in)
NOTE
The socks are worked top down from cuff to toe. Snufkin's face is embroidered following the instructions once the socks are finished.

LEG

Cast on 60 sts in yarn A and divide evenly between four needles with 15 sts on each needle. The start of the round is between needle I and needle IV at the back of the sock.

Join, being careful not to twist, and work 4cm (1½in) in rib in the round. Then knit 1 round, increasing 1 st on each needle (64 sts).

Start the Fair Isle pattern, working round 1 of chart across all 64 sts. Then work rounds 2–45 of chart. Break off yarn A and work the rest of sock in yarn B.

HEEL

Start to work heel by knitting the sts on needle I on to needle IV (32 sts for heel flap). Leave remaining sts on needles II and III. Turn work and start slip stitch pattern to reinforce heel:

Row 1 (WS): sl1 (with yarn at back of work), purl to end of row. Turn work.

Row 2 (RS): *sl1 (with yarn at back of work), k1*, repeat from * to * to end of row. Turn work.

Repeat rows 1 and 2 a total of 16 times and then knit one row (33 rows).

Start to decrease to turn the heel:

Continue in the same slip stitch pattern as before to reinforce heel. Starting with a RS row, work in pattern until there are 11 sts left on LH needle, skpo and turn work.

Sl1 purlwise, purl 10 sts on WS until there are 11 sts left on LH needle, p2tog and turn work.

Sl1 knitwise, work in pattern until there are 10 sts left on LH needle, skpo and turn work.

Continue as set working back and forth, i.e. always slip the first st of the row and skpo at the end of a RS row and p2tog at the end of a WS row. The number of sts at the sides will decrease by 1 each time, always leaving 12 sts in the centre. When you run out of side sts at the end of a WS row, k6 on RS. This point (centre back) is now the start of the round.

FOOT

Knit 6 sts on LH needle from heel (needle I). Using a spare needle, pick up 16 sts from LH edge of heel flap + 1 st between heel flap and needle II. Knit picked up sts on to needle I, turning sts knitwise. Knit sts on needle II and needle III. Using the needle with 6 sts on it, pick up 16 sts from RH edge of heel flap + 1 st between heel flap and needle III. Knit picked up sts and 6 sts from heel on to needle IV, turning picked up sts knitwise. You now have 78 sts.

Continue in stocking (stockinette) stitch, decreasing for gusset as follows: k2tog at end of needle I and skpo at beginning of needle IV. Work this decrease on every alt round until there are 64 stitches left, 16 on each needle.

Work in stocking (stockinette) stitch until the foot of the sock measures approximately 22cm (8¾in) or covers the wearer's little toe.

Continue in stocking (stockinette) stitch and start to work a star toe: k2tog in the middle and at the end of each needle. You will have decreased 8 sts and now have 56 sts. Work 6 rounds without decreasing and then repeat the decrease round = 48 sts. Work 5 rounds without decreasing and then repeat the decrease round = 40 sts.

Continue decreasing in this way, i.e. working one fewer rounds between decrease rounds each time. When there are 8 sts left, break off yarn and thread through remaining stitches. Pull tight and weave in ends securely.

SECOND SOCK

Work the other sock in the same way.

FINISHING

Divide yarn B into two strands and embroider Snufkin's face using short backstitches. Work French knots in yarn B for the pupils.

Weave in ends. Carefully wet socks, place on a flat surface and block to measurements. Leave to dry. Steam block lightly if necessary.

☐ = knit (yarn A)
■ = knit (yarn B)
▨ = embroider in backstitch in yarn B
◉ = French knot in yarn B

Chart

Work rounds 1–45

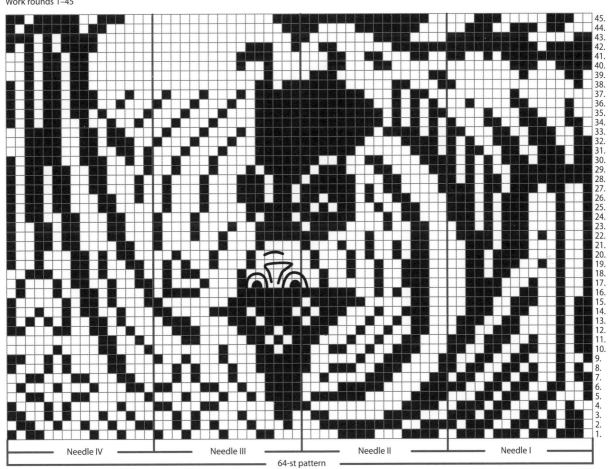

Needle IV   Needle III   Needle II   Needle I

64-st pattern

THE MOOMIN HOUSE

These socks designed by Sonja Nykänen feature an impressive mock cable cuff that looks like a tiled roof. These cheery socks are knitted using traditional Fair Isle technique and have a reinforced heel and a barn toe. The centres of the flowers that decorate the foot are embroidered on afterwards.

DESIGNER Sonja Nykänen

SIZE UK 3½/4 (Europe 36/37, US Women's 6/6½, US Men's 4/5)

YARN
1 ball each of Novita Muumitalo (Moomin House) DK (8-ply/light worsted) yarn in Moomintroll 007 (A), Snork 152 (B), Snufkin 381 (C) and a small amount of yarn in Fillyjonk 599 (D), Snorkmaiden 507 (E) and Miffle 229 (F) for the embroidery; 100g/3½oz/225m/246yd

AMOUNT USED
50g (1¾oz) of yarns A and B, 100g (3½oz) of yarn C and 25g (1oz) of yarns E and F

KNITTING NEEDLES
3mm (UK 11, US 2/3) double-pointed needles or size to obtain correct tension (gauge)

TECHNIQUES

Mock cable in the round:
Follow chart and instructions

Stocking (stockinette) stitch in the round:
Knit all rounds.

Fair Isle in the round:
Work in stocking (stockinette) stitch following chart and instructions. Catch in any floats longer than 4 sts by twisting the yarns around each other at the back of the work. Vary where you catch your floats in the design so they don't land in the same place on consecutive rounds.

TENSION (GAUGE) 24 sts in Fair Isle = 10cm (4in)

NOTE

The socks are worked top down from cuff to toe. The porch roof and the centres of the flowers are embroidered on afterwards in duplicate stitch.

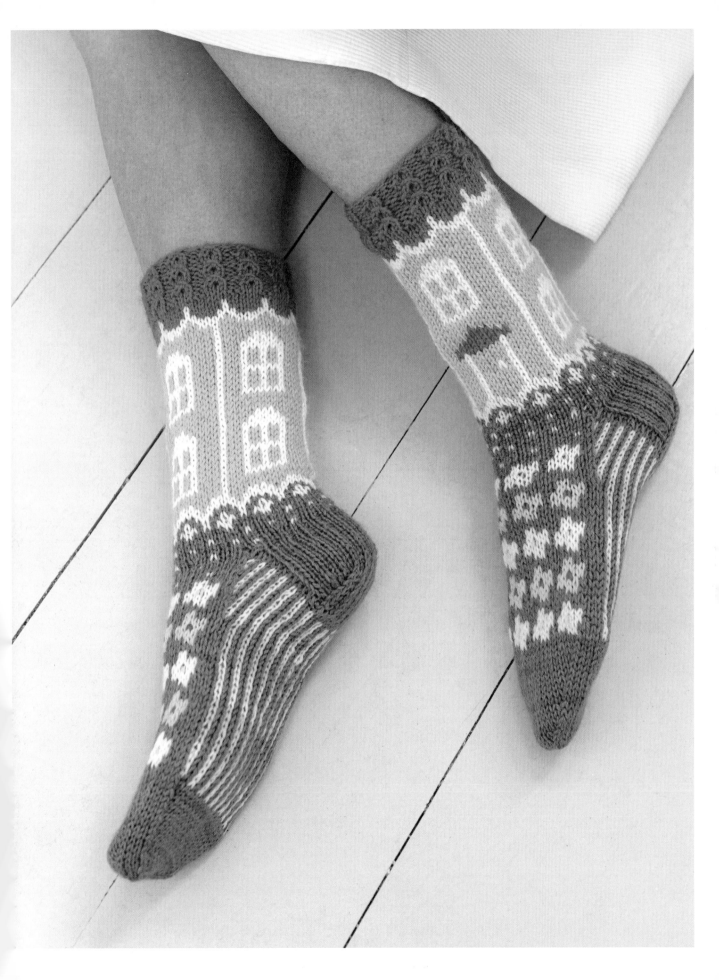

LEG

Cast on 60 sts in yarn D and divide evenly between four needles with 15 sts on each needle. The start of the round is between needle I and needle IV at the back of the sock.

Join, being careful not to twist, and start working mock cable pattern in the round from round 1 of Chart I repeating the 5-st pattern 12 times. Repeat rounds 1–4 of chart three times in total. Then knit one round.

Start the Fair Isle pattern, working round 1 of Chart II across all 60 sts. Then work rounds 2–41 of chart. **Note:** knit the porch roof in yarn A first and embroider over the top in duplicate stitch in yarn D at the end. On round 41, decrease on each needle as shown on chart (56 sts).

Work rounds 42–46 of chart and decrease on each needle as shown on chart on the last round (52 sts).

HEEL

Work the heel in yarn C.

Start to work heel by knitting the sts on needle I on to needle IV (26 sts for heel flap). Leave remaining sts on needles II and III. Turn work and start slip stitch pattern to reinforce heel:

Row 1 (WS): sl1 (with yarn at back of work), purl to end of row. Turn work.

Row 2 (RS): *sl1 (with yarn at back of work), k1*, repeat from * to * to end of row. Turn work.

Repeat rows 1 and 2 a total of 13 times and then knit one row (27 rows).

Start to decrease to turn the heel:

Continue in the same slip stitch pattern as before to reinforce heel. Starting with a RS row, sl1 knitwise, work in pattern until there are 9 sts left on LH needle, skpo and turn work.

Chart I

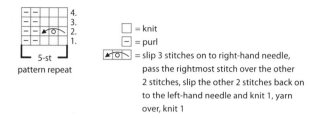

= knit

= purl

= slip 3 stitches on to right-hand needle, pass the rightmost stitch over the other 2 stitches, slip the other 2 stitches back on to the left-hand needle and knit 1, yarn over, knit 1

WS row: sl1, purl 8 sts until there are 9 sts left on LH needle, p2tog and turn work.

RS row: sl1 knitwise, work in pattern until there are 8 sts left on LH needle, skpo and turn work.

Continue as set working back and forth, i.e. always slip the first st of the row and skpo at the end of a RS row and p2tog at the end of a WS row. The number of sts at the sides will decrease by 1 each time, always leaving 10 sts in the centre. When you run out of side sts at the end of a WS row, k5 on RS. This point (centre back) is now the start of the round.

FOOT

Using needle I, pick up 13 sts from LH edge of heel flap + 1 st between heel flap and needle II. Using needle IV, pick up 13 sts from RH edge of heel flap + 1 st between heel flap and needle III. You now have 64 sts.

Start the Fair Isle pattern for the foot, working round 1 of chart III. Knit stitches picked up from edge of heel flap on to needle I through back loops and knit remaining sts as normal. Then work rounds 2–34 of chart. Work gusset decreases as shown in chart: k2tog at end of needle I and skpo at beginning of needle IV. Work this decrease on every alt round until there are 52 sts left. **Note:** embroider the centres of the flowers in duplicate stitch as you go.

Chart II

Work rounds 1–46

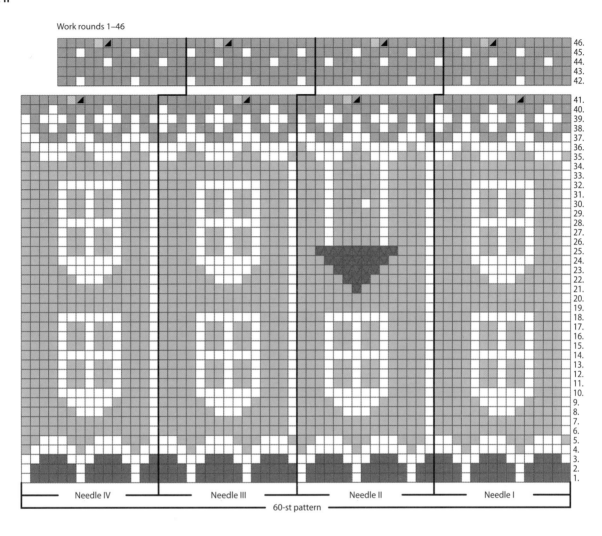

Needle IV — Needle III — Needle II — Needle I

60-st pattern

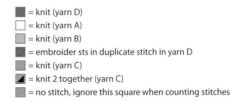

■ = knit (yarn D)
□ = knit (yarn A)
▨ = knit (yarn B)
■ = embroider sts in duplicate stitch in yarn D
▨ = knit (yarn C)
◤ = knit 2 together (yarn C)
▨ = no stitch, ignore this square when counting stitches

Break off other yarns and finish sock in yarn C. If necessary, work additional rounds in stocking (stockinette) stitch in yarn C until the foot of the sock covers the wearer's little toe.

Continue in stocking (stockinette) stitch and start to decrease for barn toe:

Needle I and needle III: work to last 3 sts, k2tog, k1.

Needle II and needle IV: k1, skpo, work to end.

Decrease as set on every alt round until there are 24 sts left and then work decreases on every round until there are 8 sts left. Break yarn and thread through remaining sts.

SECOND SOCK

Work other sock in the same way but swap the positions of the door and the middle window at the bottom so the socks are a mirror image of each other.

FINISHING

Weave in ends. Carefully wet socks, place on a flat surface and block to measurements. Leave to dry. Steam block lightly if necessary.

Chart III

Work rounds 1–34

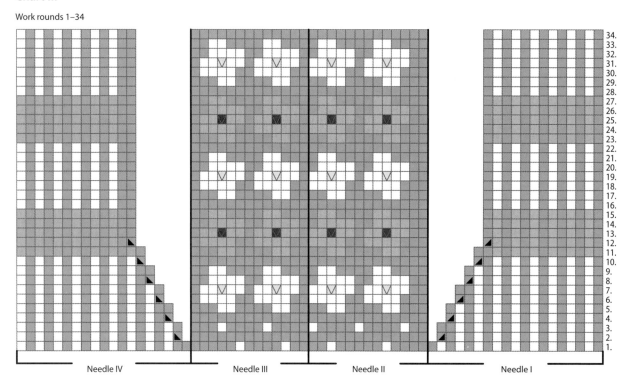

Needle IV	Needle III	Needle II	Needle I

 = knit (yarn C)

☐ = knit (yarn A)

▨ = knit (yarn E)

☑ = embroider sts in duplicate stitch in yarn B

◼ = embroider sts in duplicate stitch in yarn D

◣ = slip 1 stitch knitwise, knit 1 in yarn C and pass the slipped stitch over the knitted stitch

◢ = knit 2 together (yarn C)

84

'And so the Moominhouse was rather full – a place where everyone did what they liked and seldom worried about tomorrow.'

Finn Family Moomintroll

THE INVISIBLE CHILD

Pale pink and bright red are the palette for these Invisible Child socks. Invisible Ninny is on the front of the leg and the sides are decorated with climbing roses. Marita Karlsson has designed these socks with a twisted rib cuff.

DESIGNER Marita Karlsson

SIZES UK 5/6(6½/7½) (Europe 38/39(40/41), US Women's 7½/8½(9/10), US Men's 6/7(7½/8½))

YARN

2 balls of Novita Muumitalo (Moomin House) DK (8-ply/light worsted) yarn in Snorkmaiden 507 (A) and 1 ball in Fillyjonk 599 (B); 100g/3½oz/225m/246yd

AMOUNT USED

150g (5½oz) of yarn A and 100g (3½oz) of yarn B for both sizes

KNITTING NEEDLES

3mm (UK 11, US 2/3) double-pointed needles or size to obtain correct tension (gauge)

TECHNIQUES

Twisted rib in the round:
knit 1 twisted, i.e. through back loop, purl 1, repeat from * to *.

Stocking (stockinette) stitch in the round:
Knit all rounds.

Fair Isle in the round:
Work in stocking (stockinette) stitch following chart and instructions. Catch in any floats longer than 4 sts by twisting the yarns around each other at the back of the work. Vary where you catch your floats in the design so they don't land in the same place on consecutive rounds.

TENSION (GAUGE) 29 sts in Fair Isle = 10cm (4in)

NOTE

The socks are worked top down from cuff to toe.

LEG

Cast on 72(76) sts in yarn B and divide evenly between four needles with 18(19) sts on each needle. The start of the round is between needle I and needle IV at the back of the sock.

Join, being careful not to twist, and work 4.5cm (1¾in) in twisted rib in the round. Knit 1 round in yarn A, decreasing 4 sts evenly across round (68(72) sts). For the larger size, divide sts between needles as follows: 19 sts on needles I and IV and 17 sts on needles II and III.

Start the Fair Isle pattern, working round 1 of the chart across all 68(72) sts. Then work rounds 2–40 of chart. Decrease at places marked on chart. **Note:** when following the instructions for the larger size, always treat the decrease st for the smaller size as a knit st and work it in the yarn as shown by the colour of the square.

Once you have completed the chart, you will have 62(66) sts. Break off yarn B and work the rest of the sock in yarn A. Continue in stocking (stockinette) stitch, decreasing as follows:

Next round: k2tog at beginning of round and ssk at end of round (60(64) sts).

Next round: decrease 4 sts evenly across round (56(60) sts).

Work two rounds with no decreases.

Next round: k2tog at beginning of round and ssk at end of round (54(58) sts).

Work three rounds with no decreases.

Next round: k2tog at start of round and ssk at end of round (52(56) sts).

Work 2cm (¾in) with no decreases.

Divide sts evenly with 13(14) sts on each needle.

HEEL

Start to work heel by knitting the sts on needle I on to needle IV = 26(28) sts for heel flap. Leave remaining sts on needles II and III.

Turn work and start slip stitch pattern to reinforce heel:

Row 1 (WS): sl1 (with yarn at back of work), purl to end of row. Turn work.

Row 2 (RS): *sl1 (with yarn at back of work), k1*, repeat from * to * to end of row. Turn work.

Repeat rows 1 and 2 a total of 13(14) times and then work row 1 again (27(29) rows).

Start to work a French heel (rounded heel):

Row 1 (RS): sl1 (with yarn at back of work), k14(15), ssk, k1. Turn work.

Row 2 (WS): sl1 purlwise, p5, p2tog, p1. Turn work.

Row 3: sl1 knitwise, k6, ssk, k1. Turn work.

Row 4: sl1 purlwise, p7, p2tog, p1. Turn work.

Continue decreasing in this way, increasing the number of sts in the centre by one on each row until all sts at the sides have been decreased. Then work one more WS row. **Note:** for the larger size, there will be no stitch left to k1/ p1 at the end of the row after the last decrease.

Turn work. Divide heel sts evenly between two needles with 8 sts on each needle. Knit sts on RH needle. This point (centre back) is now the start of the round.

FOOT

Knit the 8 sts on LH needle from heel (needle I). Using a spare needle, pick up 14(15) sts from LH edge of heel flap + 1 st between heel flap and needle II. Knit picked up sts on to needle I, turning sts knitwise. Knit sts on needle II and needle III. Using the needle with 8 sts on it, pick up 14(15) sts from RH edge of heel flap + 1 st between heel flap and needle III. Knit picked up sts and 8 sts from heel on to needle IV, turning picked up sts knitwise. You now have 72(76) sts.

Continue in stocking (stockinette) stitch, decreasing for gusset as follows: k2tog at end of needle I and ssk at beginning of needle IV. Repeat decreases on every alt round until there are 13(14) sts left on each needle.

Continue in stocking (stockinette) stitch until the foot of the sock measures approximately 20.5(22)cm / 8(8¾)in or covers the wearer's little toe.

Start to decrease to work a wedge toe:

Needle I and needle III: work to last 3 sts, k2tog, k1.

Needle II and needle IV: k1, ssk, work to end.

Decrease as set on every alt round until there are 36 sts left and then work decreases on every round until there are 16 sts left.

Divide remaining sts evenly between two needles with 8 sts on the upper needle and 8 sts on the lower needle. Graft sts together. There are instructions and videos available online showing how to graft (sometimes called Kitchener stitch).

SECOND SOCK

Work the other sock in the same way.

FINISHING

Weave in ends. Carefully wet socks, place on a flat surface and block to measurements. Leave to dry. Steam block lightly if necessary.

= knit (yarn A)

= knit (yarn B)

smaller size only { = slip, slip, knit decrease (yarn A)
{ = knit 2 together (yarn A)

larger size only { = slip, slip, knit decrease (yarn A)
{ = knit 2 together (yarn A)

Chart

Work rounds 1–40

End of needle III, beginning of needle IV

End of needle II, beginning of needle III

End of needle I, beginning of needle II

68-st pattern (smaller size)

72-st pattern (larger size)

RAMBLING ROSES

Minttu Wikberg designed these socks around Moominmamma's love of roses. Beneath the initials 'MM', the legs of the socks are decorated with beautiful, trailing roses. These knee-length socks are knitted using the traditional Fair Isle technique and the heel is inserted at the end.

DESIGNER Minttu Wikberg

SIZE UK 5 (Europe 38, US Women's 7½, US Men's 6)

YARN

1 ball each of Novita Muumitalo (Moomin House) DK (8-ply/light worsted) yarn in Moomintroll 007 (A), Fillyjonk 599 (B) and Stinky 099 (C); 100g/3½oz/225m/246yd

AMOUNT USED

100g (3½oz) of yarns A and B and 50g (1¾oz) of yarn C

KNITTING NEEDLES

3mm (UK 11, US 2/3) double-pointed needles or size to obtain correct tension (gauge)

TECHNIQUES

Twisted rib in the round:
knit 1 twisted, i.e. through back loop, purl 1, repeat from * to *.

Stocking (stockinette) stitch in the round:
Knit all rounds.

Fair Isle in the round:
Work in stocking (stockinette) stitch following chart and instructions. Catch in any floats longer than 4 sts by twisting the yarns around each other at the back of the work. Vary where you catch your floats in the design so they don't land in the same place on consecutive rounds.

TENSION (GAUGE) 25 sts in Fair Isle = 10cm (4in)

NOTE

The socks are worked top down from cuff to toe. The heel is inserted and worked last.

LEG AND FOOT

Cast on 76 sts in yarn C and divide evenly between four needles with 19 sts on each needle. The start of the round is between needle I and needle IV at the side of the sock.

Join, being careful not to twist, and work 3.5cm (1⅜in) in twisted rib in the round. Then knit one round, increasing 1 st on needle I (77 sts).

Start the Fair Isle pattern at round 1 of Chart I and work all 22 rounds. Then knit one round in yarn A, decreasing 1 st on needle I (76 sts). Divide sts between needles as follows: needle I 13 sts, needle II 14 sts, needle III 25 sts and needle IV 24 sts.

Continue working in Fair Isle starting from round 1 of Chart II and working across all 76 sts. Then work rounds 2–61. Decrease at places marked on chart. You now have 56 sts. Divide sts evenly with 14 sts on each needle.

On the next round, mark the position of the inserted heel.

Work sts on needles I and II in a contrasting yarn. Break off contrasting yarn. Work sts in contrasting yarn on needles I and II again following round 62 of chart.

Work to the end of round 62 on needles III and IV and then work chart to the end. Break off yarn B. Continue in stocking (stockinette) stitch in yarn A until foot measures approximately 14cm (5½in) from the contrasting yarn to mark the heel.

Start to decrease to work barn toe:

Needle I and needle III: k1, skpo, work to end.

Needle II and needle IV: work to last 3 sts, k2tog, k1.

Decrease as set on every alt round until there are 24 sts left and then work decreases on every round until there are 8 sts left. Break yarn and thread through remaining sts.

Chart I

□ = knit (yarn A)
■ = knit (yarn C)

Work rounds 1–22

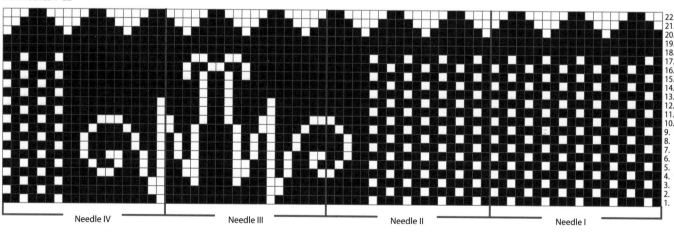

22. 21. 20. 19. 18. 17. 16. 15. 14. 13. 12. 11. 10. 9. 8. 7. 6. 5. 4. 3. 2. 1.

Needle IV   Needle III   Needle II   Needle I

Chart II

Work rounds 1–90

□ = knit (yarn A)

■ = knit (yarn B)

◢ = knit 2 together (yarn A)

◣ = knit 2 together through back loops
(yarn A)

━ = position of inserted heel

90.
89.
88.
87.
86.
85.
84.
83.
82.
81.
80.
79.
78.
77.
76.
75.
74.
73.
72.
71.
70.
69.
68.
67.
66.
65.
64.
63.
62.
61.
60.
59.
58.
57.
56.
55.
54.
53.
52.
51.
50.
49.
48.
47.
46.
45.
44.
43.
42.
41.
40.
39.
38.
37.
36.
35.
34.
33.
32.
31.
30.
29.
28.
27.
26.
25.
24.
23.
22.
21.
20.
19.
18.
17.
16.
15.
14.
13.
12.
11.
10.
9.
8.
7.
6.
5.
4.
3.
2.
1.

Needle IV — Needle III — Needle II — Needle I

76-st pattern

HEEL

Carefully remove contrasting yarn and using yarn B pick up 28 sts from above and below the hole and 2 additional sts from each side of the hole (60 sts). Place stitch markers at both edges, between the added sts. Divide sts evenly between four needles. The start of the round will be at the stitch marker at one side.

Work 1 round in stocking (stockinette) stitch in the round.

Start to decrease to turn heel:

Needle I and needle III: k1, k2tog through back loops, work to end.

Needle II and needle IV: work to last 3 sts, k2tog, k1.

Decrease as set on every alt round four more times and then on every round five times (20 sts).

Divide remaining sts evenly between two needles with 10 sts for the heel on the upper and lower needle. Graft sts together. There are instructions and videos available online showing how to graft (sometimes called Kitchener stitch).

SECOND SOCK

Work the other sock in the same way.

FINISHING

Weave in ends. Carefully wet socks, place on a flat surface and block to measurements. Leave to dry. Steam block lightly if necessary.

'Here she was at last
in her own garden
where everything was
in its proper place and
everything was growing
just as it should grow.'

Moominpappa at Sea

PRIMADONNA'S HORSE

Primadonna's horse, Moomin Valley's circus horse, peeks out from under her voluminous forelock in these socks designed by Pirjo Iivonen. They are knitted in two colours and the pink flowers and the bow are embroidered on at the end. The socks have a traditional ribbed cuff and the Fair Isle design is worked using the ladder back jacquard technique on the wrong side.

DESIGNER Pirjo Iivonen

SIZES UK 2½–6(6½–9) (Europe 35–39(40–43), US Women's 5–8½(9–11½), US Men's 3½–7(7½–10))

YARN

1 ball of Novita Muumitalo (Moomin House) DK (8-ply/ light worsted) yarn in Moomintroll 007 (A) and 2 balls in Stinky 099 (B), plus a small amount of Hemulen 720 (C) for the embroidery; 100g/3½oz/225m/246yd

AMOUNT USED

100g (3½oz) of yarn A for both sizes, 150/200g (5¼/7oz) of yarn B and 25g (1oz) of yarn C

KNITTING NEEDLES

3mm (UK 11, US 2/3) double-pointed needles or size to obtain correct tension (gauge)

TECHNIQUES

Rib in the round:
knit 2, purl 2, repeat from * to *.

Stocking (stockinette) stitch in the round:
Knit all rounds.

Fair Isle in the round:
Work in stocking (stockinette) stitch following chart and instructions. Use the ladder back jacquard technique to catch in the long floats. You can find videos and instructions showing how to do this online. The places where the ladder stitches are worked are shown on the chart.

TENSION (GAUGE) 25 sts in st st = 10cm (4in)

NOTE

The socks are worked top down from cuff to toe. Check your tension (gauge) over the Fair Isle pattern as the ladder back jacquard technique can easily make your knitting looser. The little details in yarn C are embroidered at the end following the instructions.

LEG

Cast on 64(72) sts in yarn A and divide between four needles with 16(18) sts on each needle. The start of the round is between needle I and needle IV at the back of the sock.

Join, being careful not to twist, and work 10 rounds in rib and then knit 1 round. Work round 1 of Chart I A(II A for larger size) across all 64(72) sts creating ladder sts on WS between the sts marked on the chart.

= knit (yarn A)

= knit (yarn B)

= embroider sts in duplicate stitch in yarn C

= embroider a flower in lazy daisy stitch in yarn C

= slip, slip, knit decrease (yarn B)

= knit 2 together (yarn B)

= location of ladder stitches, purl ladder sts

= make ladder st by picking up the yarn between the stitches and twisting it knitwise

Chart I A

Work rounds 1–62

Needle IV   Needle III   Needle II   Needle I

64-st pattern

98

Start the Fair Isle pattern at round 2 of chart and then work rounds 3–62. Work the sts that will be embroidered at the end in yarn B. Decrease at places marked on chart. Anchor the ladders on round 61 by knitting them together with the next st.

You now have 56(60) sts. Divide sts evenly between needles with 14(15) sts on each needle. Work the rest of the sock in yarn B.

HEEL

Start to work heel by knitting the sts on needle I on to needle IV (28(30) sts for heel flap). Leave remaining sts on needles II and III. Turn work and start slip stitch pattern to reinforce heel:

Row 1 (WS): sl1 (with yarn at back of work), purl to end of row. Turn work.

Row 2 (RS): *sl1 (with yarn at back of work), k1*, repeat from * to * to end of row. Turn work.

Repeat rows 1 and 2 a total of 14(15) times and then knit 1 row (29(31) rows).

Start to decrease to turn the heel:

Chart I B

Work rounds 1–62

Needle IV   Needle III   Needle II   Needle I

64-st pattern

99

Continue in the same slip stitch pattern as before to reinforce heel. Starting with a RS row, sl1 knitwise, work in pattern until there are 9(10) sts left on LH needle, ssk and turn work.

Sl1 purlwise, purl 10 sts on WS until there are 9(10) sts left on LH needle, p2tog and turn work.

Sl1 knitwise, work in pattern until there are 8(9) sts left on LH needle, ssk and turn work.

Continue as set working back and forth, i.e. always slip the first st of the row and ssk at the end of a RS row and p2tog at the end of a WS row. The number of sts at the sides will decrease by 1 each time, always leaving 12 sts in the centre. When you run out of side sts at the end of a WS row, k6 on RS. This point is now the start of the round.

Chart II A

Work rounds 1–62

Needle IV · Needle III · Needle II · Needle I

72-st pattern

Chart II B

Work rounds 1–62

62.
61.
60.
59.
58.
57.
56.
55.
54.
53.
52.
51.
50.
49.
48.
47.
46.
45.
44.
43.
42.
41.
40.
39.
38.
37.
36.
35.
34.
33.
32.
31.
30.
29.
28.
27.
26.
25.
24.
23.
22.
21.
20.
19.
18.
17.
16.
15.
14.
13.
12.
11.
10.
9.
8.
7.
6.
5.
4.
3.
2.
1.

Needle IV — Needle III — Needle II — Needle I

72-st pattern

 = knit (yarn A)

■ = knit (yarn B)

▼ = embroider sts in duplicate stitch in yarn C

✕ = embroider a flower in lazy daisy st in yarn C

◣ = slip, slip, knit decrease (yarn B)

◢ = knit 2 together (yarn B)

| = location of ladder stitches, purl ladder sts

● = make ladder st by picking up the yarn between the stitches
  and twisting it knitwise

FOOT

Knit 6 sts on LH needle from heel (needle I). Using a spare needle, pick up 14(15) sts from LH edge of heel flap + 1 st between heel flap and needle II. Knit picked up sts on to needle I, turning sts knitwise. Knit sts on needle II and needle III. Using the needle with 6 sts on it, pick up 14(15) sts from RH edge of heel flap + 1 st between heel flap and needle III. Knit picked up sts and 6 sts from heel on to needle IV, turning picked up sts knitwise. You now have 70(74) sts.

Continue in stocking (stockinette) stitch, decreasing for gusset as follows: k2tog at end of needle I and ssk at beginning of needle IV. Work this decrease on every alt round until there are 56(60) stitches left, 14(15) on each needle. **Note:** if you are making the socks for a narrow foot, decrease a few more times. Remember to divide sts evenly between your needles at the end.

Work in stocking (stockinette) stitch until the foot of the sock measures 5(6.5)cm / 2(2½)in shorter than the final desired length.

Continue in stocking (stockinette) stitch and start to decrease to work barn toe:

Needle I and needle III: work to last 3 sts, k2tog, k1.

Needle II and needle IV: k1, ssk, work to end.

Repeat these decreases on every alt round until there are 28 sts left and then on every round until there are 8 sts left. Break yarn and thread through remaining sts.

Work other sock in the same way but following Chart I B(II B for larger size) to knit the leg with the design reversed.

FINISHING

Embroider the bow at the neck in duplicate stitch with yarn C then bring the ends to RS. Tie the ends in a bow and knot the loops. Embroider the flowers on the horse's body using lazy daisy stitch in the positions as shown on the chart. Embroider a few flowers on the foot of the sock too.

Weave in ends. Carefully wet socks, place on a flat surface and block to measurements. Leave to dry. Steam block lightly if necessary.

"'Excuse me, but I don't drink coffee. I just eat flowers.'"

'Moomin Falls in Love', *Moomin: The Complete Tove Jansson Comic Strip Book 3*

BEWARE OF THE GROKE

These Groke socks are designed for larger feet and are lovely and warm inside a pair of boots. The knit stitches in the cuff's ribbing are worked twisted. The leg is worked using the intarsia technique in the round, and the foot is worked in Fair Isle. Add the little details with embroidery at the end.

DESIGNER Sisko Sälpäkivi

SIZES UK 8(11) (Europe 42(46), US Women's 10(13½), US Men's 9(12))

YARN

1(2) balls each of Novita Muumitalo (Moomin House) DK (8-ply/light worsted) yarn in The Ancestor 401 (A) and Stinky 099 (B), 1 ball in Moomintroll 007 (C), and a small amount of Miffle 229 or other yellow yarn (D) for the embroidery; 100g/3½oz/225m/246yd

AMOUNT USED

100(150)g (3½(5½)oz) of yarns A and B, 25g (1oz) of yarn C for both sizes and 25g (1oz) of yarn D

KNITTING NEEDLES

3mm (UK 11, US 2/3) double-pointed needles or size to obtain correct tension (gauge)

TECHNIQUES

Twisted rib in the round:
knit 1 through back loop, purl 1, repeat from * to *.

Stocking (stockinette) stitch in the round:
Knit all rounds.

Fair Isle in the round:
Work in stocking (stockinette) stitch following chart and instructions.

Intarsia in the round:
Knit on RS and purl on WS following instructions. Use a separate ball of wool for each section of colour and twist the different coloured yarns around each other at back of work where the two meet so as not to form holes.

TENSION (GAUGE) 25 sts in st st = 10cm (4in)

NOTE

The socks are worked top down from cuff to toe. Work the Groke and the background using the intarsia technique in the round and embroider the details (the outlines of the clouds and the ground, the stars, mouth and eyes) at the end. Alternatively, work the leg in rows using the intarsia technique. If using this method, add 1 st at each edge to act as a seam allowance and decrease these sts before working the heel.

LEFT SOCK

Cast on 66(70) sts in yarn A and divide between four needles with 17(18) sts on needles I and IV and 16(17) sts on needles II and III. The start of the round is between needle I and needle IV at the back of the sock.

Join, being careful not to twist, and work 3cm (1¼in) in twisted rib in the round. Then knit one round, increasing 1 st on each needle (70(74) sts). Divide sts between needles as follows: 19(21) sts on needles I and IV and 16(16) sts on needles II and III.

Start the intarsia pattern in the round, working round 1 of Chart I A across all 70(74) sts. *Turn work, yarn over and purl next round of chart. At end of round purl last st of round and the yarn over from the beginning of the round together. Turn work, yarn over and knit next round of chart. Work the yarn over from the beginning of the round and the last st together using skpo.* Repeat from * to * and work all rounds of chart.

Note: work the Groke and the background using the intarsia technique and embroider the details (the outlines of the clouds and the ground, the stars, mouth and eyes) at the end. Work the places where stitches will be embroidered in either yarn A or yarn B.

Decrease on rounds 27, 41, 57 and 67 of chart as follows: at beginning of round yarn over, k2tog, work to last 3 sts in round, skpo, and then work the yarn over from the beginning of the round and the last st together using skpo. **Note:** when following the instructions for the larger size, always treat the decrease st for the smaller size as a knit st and work it in the yarn as shown by the colour of the square.

Once you have completed the chart, you will have 62(66) sts. Divide sts between needles as follows: 15(17) sts on needles I and IV and 16(16) sts on needles II and III.

HEEL

Work heel in yarn A.

Start to work heel by knitting the sts on needle I on to needle IV. For larger size also decrease 2 sts evenly (30(32) sts for heel flap). Leave remaining sts on needles II and III. Turn work and start slip stitch pattern to reinforce heel:

Row 1 (WS): sl1 (with yarn at back of work), purl to end of row. Turn work.

Row 2 (RS): *sl1 (with yarn at back of work), k1*, repeat from * to * to end of row. Turn work.

Repeat rows 1 and 2 a total of 15(16) times and then knit 1 row (31(33) rows).

Start to decrease to turn the heel:

Continue in the same slip stitch pattern as before to reinforce heel. Starting with a RS row, work in pattern until there are 11(12) sts left on LH needle, skpo and turn work.

Sl1 purlwise and purl 8 sts on WS until there are 11(12) sts left on LH needle. P2tog and turn work.

Sl1 knitwise, work in pattern until there are 10(11) sts left on LH needle, skpo and turn work.

Continue as set working back and forth, i.e. always slip the first st of the row and skpo at the end of a RS row and p2tog at the end of a WS row. The number of sts at the sides will decrease by 1 each time, always leaving 10 sts in the centre. When you run out of side sts at the end of a WS row, k5 on RS. This point (centre back) is now the start of the round.

Chart I A

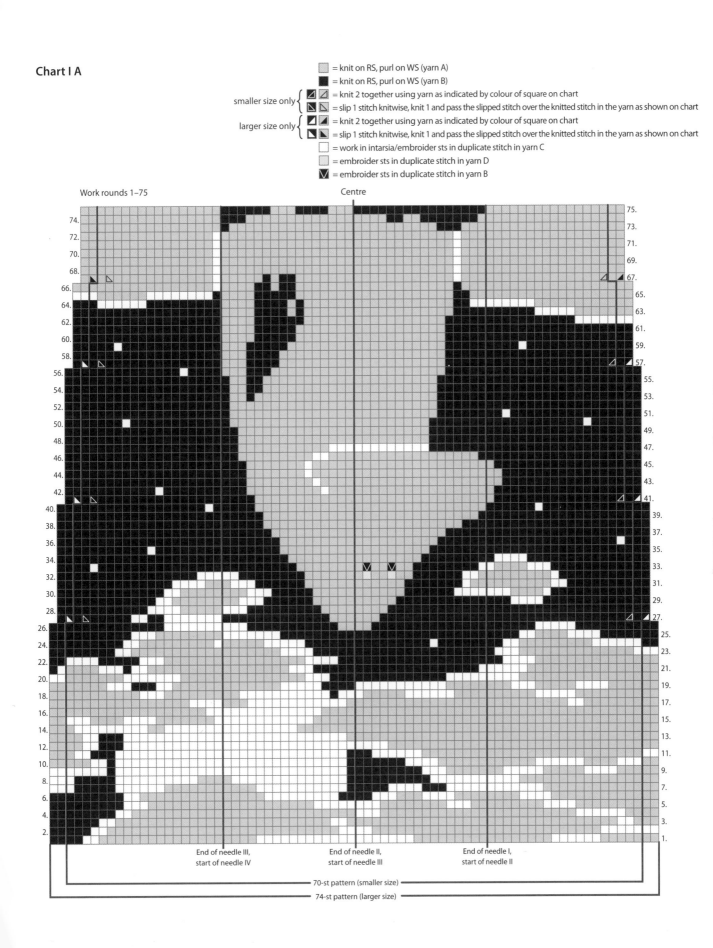

Legend:
- = knit on RS, purl on WS (yarn A)
- = knit on RS, purl on WS (yarn B)

smaller size only {
- = knit 2 together using yarn as indicated by colour of square on chart
- = slip 1 stitch knitwise, knit 1 and pass the slipped stitch over the knitted stitch in the yarn as shown on chart
}

larger size only {
- = knit 2 together using yarn as indicated by colour of square on chart
- = slip 1 stitch knitwise, knit 1 and pass the slipped stitch over the knitted stitch in the yarn as shown on chart
}

- = work in intarsia/embroider sts in duplicate stitch in yarn C
- = embroider sts in duplicate stitch in yarn D
- V = embroider sts in duplicate stitch in yarn B

Work rounds 1–75

Centre

End of needle III, start of needle IV

End of needle II, start of needle III

End of needle I, start of needle II

70-st pattern (smaller size)

74-st pattern (larger size)

Chart I B

= knit on RS, purl on WS (yarn A)

= knit on RS, purl on WS (yarn B)

smaller size only { = knit 2 together using yarn as indicated by colour of square on chart

= slip 1 stitch knitwise, knit 1 and pass the slipped stitch over the knitted stitch in the yarn as shown on chart

larger size only { = knit 2 together using yarn as indicated by colour of square on chart

= slip 1 stitch knitwise, knit 1 and pass the slipped stitch over the knitted stitch in the yarn as shown on chart

= work in intarsia/embroider sts in duplicate stitch in yarn C

= embroider sts in duplicate stitch in yarn D

= embroider sts in duplicate stitch in yarn B

Work rounds 1–75

Centre

End of needle III, start of needle IV

End of needle II, start of needle III

End of needle I, start of needle II

70-st pattern (smaller size)

74-st pattern (larger size)

FOOT

Using needle I, pick up 15(16) sts from LH edge of heel flap + 1 st between heel flap and needle II. Using needle IV, pick up 15(16) sts from RH edge of heel flap + 1 st between heel flap and needle III. You now have 74(76) sts.

Start the Fair Isle pattern at round 1 of Chart II A. Knit stitches picked up from edge of heel flap on to needle I through back loops and knit remaining sts as normal. Then work rounds 2–15 of chart. Work gusset decreases as shown in chart: k2tog at end of needle I and skpo at beginning of needle IV. Work this decrease on every alt round until there are 60(62) sts left. Divide sts between needles as follows. 14(15) sts on needles I and IV and 16(16) sts on needles II and III.

Now repeat rounds 16–19 of Chart II A until the foot of the sock measures 22(25)cm / 8¾(9¾)in or covers the wearer's little toe. Break off yarn A and work toe in yarn B. For larger size, knit 1 more round, decreasing 2 sts on sole of foot. Divide sts evenly with 15 sts on each needle.

Continue in stocking (stockinette) stitch and start to decrease to work barn toe:

Needle I and needle III: work to last 3 sts, k2tog, k1.

Needle II and needle IV: k1, skpo, work to end.

Repeat these decreases on every alt round until there are 28 sts left and then on every round until there are 8 sts left. Break yarn and thread through remaining sts.

RIGHT SOCK

Work other sock as a mirror image following Charts I B and II B.

FINISHING

Embroider the stars, the white outlines of the clouds and the land and the Groke's mouth in yarn C using duplicate stitch. Embroider the eyes in yarns B and D using duplicate stitch.

Weave in ends. Carefully wet socks, place on a flat surface and block to measurements. Leave to dry. Steam block lightly if necessary.

Chart II A

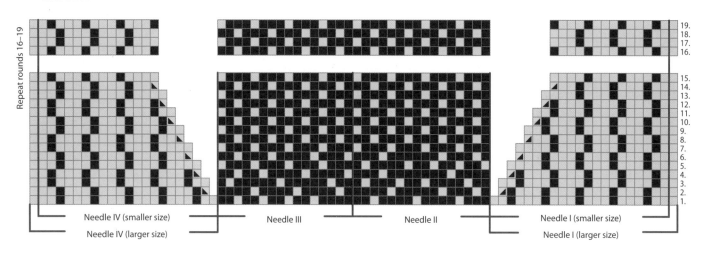

Chart II B

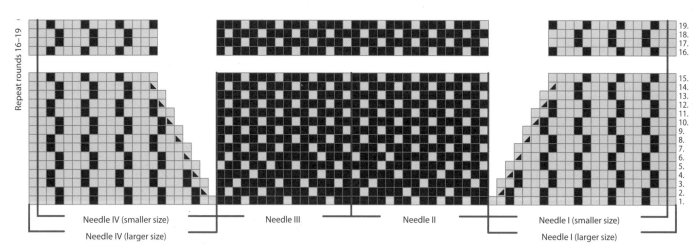

☐ = knit (yarn A)
■ = knit (yarn B)
◢ = knit 2 together (yarn A)
◥ = slip 1 stitch knitwise, knit 1 in yarn A and pass the slipped stitch over the knitted stitch

'He looked quickly out over the ice and thought he could see
the big, clumsy Groke shuffling along somewhere near the horizon.'

Moominland Midwinter

ROMANTIC MOOMINS

In these socks, Moomintroll and Snorkmaiden watch the sunset together. The cuffs have a picot edge and the Fair Isle design is worked using the ladder back jacquard technique. The outlines of the Moomins and the little details are embroidered on afterwards.

DESIGNER Pirjo Iivonen

SIZES UK 2½–6(6½–9) (Europe 35–39(40–43), US Women's 5–8½(9–11½), US Men's 3½–7(7½-10))

YARN

1 ball each of Novita Muumitalo (Moomin House) DK (8-ply/light worsted) yarn in Hemulen 720 (A), Moomintroll 007 (B), The Ancestor 401 (C), Snork 152 (D) and a small amount of Stinky 099 (E) for the embroidery; 100g/3½oz/225m/246yd

AMOUNT USED

100g (3½oz) of yarns A, B and D, 50g (1¾oz) of yarn C for both sizes and 25g (1oz) of yarn E

KNITTING NEEDLES

3mm (UK 11, US 2/3) double-pointed needles or size to obtain correct tension (gauge)

TECHNIQUES

Stocking (stockinette) stitch in the round:
Knit all rounds.

Fair Isle in the round:
Work in stocking (stockinette) stitch following chart and instructions. Use the ladder back jacquard technique to catch in the long floats in the Fair Isle pattern on the leg. You can find videos and instructions showing how to do this online. The places where the ladder stitches are worked are shown on the chart.

TENSION (GAUGE) 25 sts in st st = 10cm (4in)

NOTE

The socks are worked top down from cuff to toe. Check your tension (gauge) over the Fair Isle pattern as the ladder back jacquard technique can easily make your knitting looser. Embroider the waves, the details on the sandy beach and the Moomin outlines following the instructions once the sock is complete.

LEG

Cast on 64(72) sts in yarn A and divide between four needles with 16(18) sts on each needle. The start of the round is between needle I and needle IV at the back of the sock.

Join, being careful not to twist, and work 5 rounds in stocking (stockinette) stitch in the round. Then work a round with holes to form the picot edge: *k2tog, yarn over*, repeat from * to * to the end of the round. Work another 5 rounds in stocking (stockinette) stitch.

Turn the top of the sock to the WS at the row of holes. Using the LH needle, pick up 1 st from the cast-on round and knit the 2 sts together (= cast-on st and the first st on the needle). Continue joining the rows of stitches along the whole round, always picking up the next stitch from the cast-on round and knitting it together with the next stitch on the LH needle.

Knit 1 round. Then work round 1 of the chart across all 64(72) sts creating ladder sts on WS between the sts marked on the chart.

Start the Fair Isle pattern at round 2 of chart and then work rounds 3–33.

At round 34 add in yarn C as shown on chart and continue the ladder back jacquard technique using three yarns on rounds 34–37. Work ladder sts using two colours together. Anchor the ladders on round 38 by knitting them together with the next st.

Then work to end of chart, decreasing as marked on chart. **Note:** when following the instructions for the larger size, always treat the decrease st for the smaller size as a knit st and work it in the yarn as shown by the colour of the square.

You now have 56(64) sts. Divide sts evenly between needles with 14(16) sts on each needle. Work the rest of the sock in yarn D.

HEEL

Start to work heel by knitting the sts on needle I on to needle IV (28(32) sts for heel flap). Leave remaining sts on needles II and III. Turn work and start slip stitch pattern to reinforce heel:

Row 1 (WS): sl1 (with yarn at back of work), purl to end of row. Turn work.

Row 2 (RS): *sl1 (with yarn at back of work), k1*, repeat from * to * to end of row. Turn work.

Repeat rows 1 and 2 a total of 14(16) times and then knit one row (29(33) rows).

Start to decrease to turn the heel:

Continue in the same slip stitch pattern as before to reinforce heel. Starting with a RS row, sl1 knitwise, work in pattern until there are 9(11) sts left on LH needle, ssk and turn work.

Sl1 purlwise, purl 10 sts on WS until there are 9(11) sts left on LH needle, p2tog and turn work.

Sl1 knitwise, work in pattern until there are 8(10) sts left on LH needle, ssk and turn work.

Continue as set working back and forth, i.e. always slip the first st of the row and ssk at the end of a RS row and p2tog at the end of a WS row. The number of sts at the sides will decrease by 1 each time, always leaving 12 sts in the centre. When you run out of side sts at the end of a WS row, k6 on RS. This point (centre back) is now the start of the round.

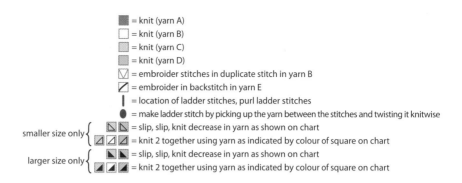

= knit (yarn A)
= knit (yarn B)
= knit (yarn C)
= knit (yarn D)
= embroider stitches in duplicate stitch in yarn B
= embroider in backstitch in yarn E
= location of ladder stitches, purl ladder stitches
= make ladder stitch by picking up the yarn between the stitches and twisting it knitwise

smaller size only { = slip, slip, knit decrease in yarn as shown on chart
= knit 2 together using yarn as indicated by colour of square on chart

larger size only { = slip, slip, knit decrease in yarn as shown on chart
= knit 2 together using yarn as indicated by colour of square on chart

Chart

Work rounds 1–56

64-st pattern (smaller size)

72-st pattern (larger size)

FOOT

Knit 6 sts on LH needle from heel (needle I). Using a spare needle, pick up 14(16) sts from LH edge of heel flap + 1 st between heel flap and needle II. Knit picked up sts on to needle I, turning sts knitwise. Knit sts on needle II and needle III. Using the needle with 6 sts on it, pick up 14(16) sts from RH edge of heel flap + 1 st between heel flap and needle III. Knit picked up sts and 6 sts from heel on to needle IV, turning picked up sts knitwise. You now have 70(78) sts.

Continue in stocking (stockinette) stitch, decreasing for gusset as follows: k2tog at end of needle I and ssk at beginning of needle IV. Work this decrease on every alt round until there are 56(64) stitches left, 14(16) on each needle. **Note:** if you are making the socks for a narrow foot, decrease a few more times. Remember to divide sts evenly between your needles at the end.

Work in stocking (stockinette) stitch until the foot of the sock measures 5(6.5)cm / 2(2½)in shorter than the final desired length.

Continue in stocking (stockinette) stitch and start to decrease to work star toe: k2tog in the middle and at the end of each needle. You will have decreased 8 sts on this round. Work 5(6) rounds without decreasing and then repeat the decrease round. Work 4(5) rounds without decreasing and then repeat the decrease round.

Continue decreasing in this way, i.e. working one fewer rounds between decrease rounds each time. When there are 8 sts left (or 12 sts if you worked a different number of gusset decreases and there were 13/15 sts on each needle before toe decreases), break off yarn and thread through remaining stitches. Pull tight and weave in ends securely.

SECOND SOCK

Work the other sock in the same way.

FINISHING

Embroider a few waves in the water in duplicate stitch using yarn B. Using yarn B, embroider the details on the sandy beach and the Moomins' tails as shown on the chart in duplicate stitch. Work a few stitches for the ends of the tails. Divide yarn E into two strands and embroider the outlines in backstitch.

Weave in ends. Carefully wet socks, place on a flat surface and block to measurements. Leave to dry. Steam block lightly if necessary.

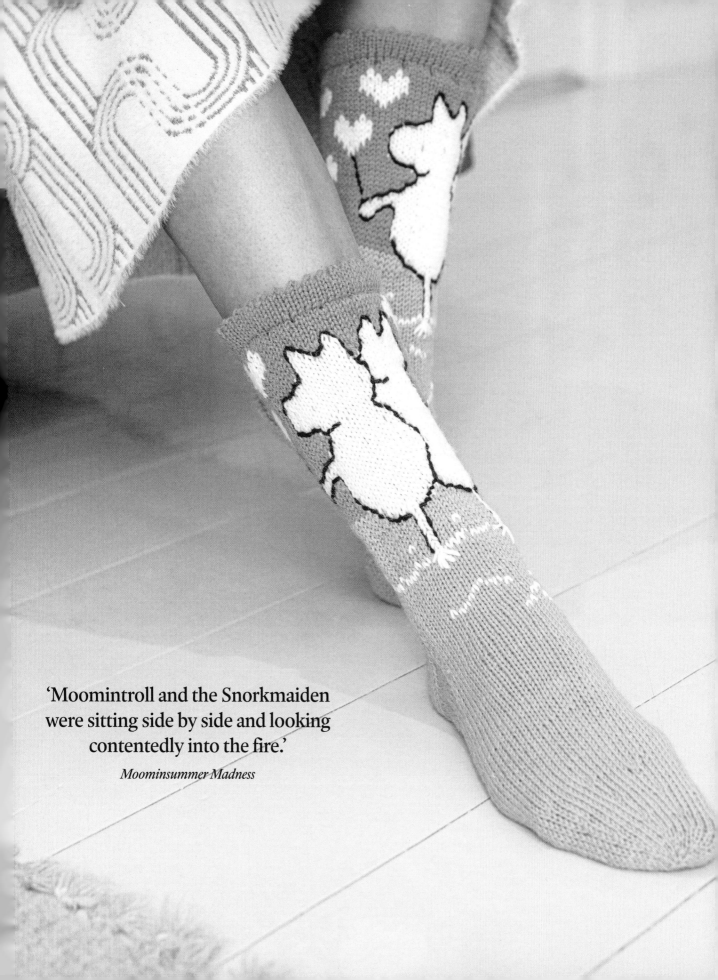

'Moomintroll and the Snorkmaiden were sitting side by side and looking contentedly into the fire.'

Moominsummer Madness

A SUMMER'S DAY

A beautiful blue sky has encouraged Moomintroll outside to sit on the grass. The designs on these socks are mainly worked in Fair Isle, but the little details are embroidered on at the end. Designed by Sonja Nykänen, these socks have a reinforced heel and a barn toe.

DESIGNER Sonja Nykänen

SIZE UK 2½/3½ (Europe 35/36, US Women's 5/6, US Men's 3½/4)

YARN

1 ball each of Novita Muumitalo (Moomin House) DK (8-ply/light worsted) yarn in Moomintroll 007 (A), Snork 152 (B) and Snufkin 381 (C), and small amounts of Hemulen 720 (D), Miffle 229 (E) and Stinky 099 (F) for the embroidery; 100g/3½oz/225m/246yd

AMOUNT USED

50g (1¾oz) of yarns A, B and C and 25g (1oz) of yarns E and F

KNITTING NEEDLES

3mm (UK 11, US 2/3) double-pointed needles or size to obtain correct tension (gauge)

TECHNIQUES

Twisted rib in the round:
knit 1 through back loop, purl 1, repeat from * to *.

Stocking (stockinette) stitch in the round:
Knit all rounds.

Fair Isle in the round:
Work in stocking (stockinette) stitch following chart and instructions. Catch in any floats longer than 3 sts by twisting the yarns around each other on the wrong side. Vary where you catch your floats in the design so they don't land in the same place on consecutive rounds.

TENSION (GAUGE) 24 sts in Fair Isle = 10cm (4in)

NOTE

The socks are worked top down from cuff to toe. Embroider the outline around Moomintroll and the centres of the flowers afterwards using duplicate stitch and backstitch. Divide the yarn into two strands to sew the outline around Moomintroll.

LEG

Cast on 56 sts in yarn A and divide evenly between four needles with 14 sts on each needle. The start of the round is between needle I and needle IV at the back of the sock.

Join, being careful not to twist, and work 3cm (1¼in) in twisted rib in the round. Then knit 1 round.

Start the Fair Isle pattern, working round 1 of Chart I A across all 56 sts. Then work rounds 2–39 of chart.

Note: the last 5 rounds of Moomintroll are worked in yarns B and C following the background pattern and the white stitches are embroidered on top at the end in yarn A using duplicate stitch.

Knit 1 round in yarn C, decreasing 4 sts evenly across round (52 sts).

Start working Fair Isle design from round 1 of Chart II: work 1 st at right side, then repeat the 6-st pattern repeat eight times and finally knit the 3 sts at the left side. Then work rounds 2–6 of chart. **Note:** work the centres of the flowers in yarn C and embroider over the top in yarn E afterwards with duplicate stitch.

Chart II

Work rounds 1–6

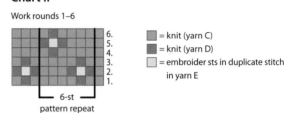

6.
5.
4.
3.
2.
1.

6-st
pattern repeat

■ = knit (yarn C)
■ = knit (yarn D)
□ = embroider sts in duplicate stitch
    in yarn E

□ = knit (yarn A)
▨ = knit (yarn B)
▨ = knit (yarn C)
▽ = embroider sts in duplicate stitch in yarn A
▧ = embroider in backstitch in yarn E

Chart I A

Work rounds 1–39

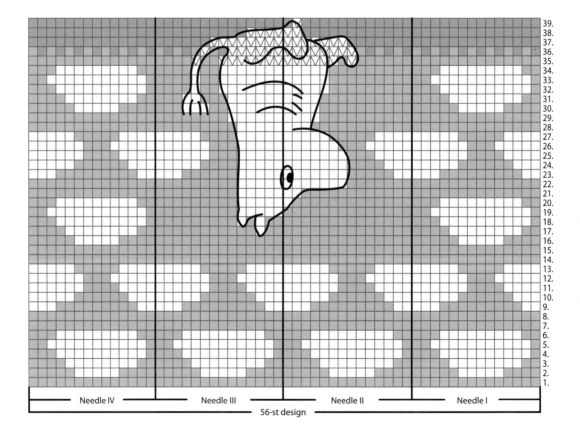

39.
38.
37.
36.
35.
34.
33.
32.
31.
30.
29.
28.
27.
26.
25.
24.
23.
22.
21.
20.
19.
18.
17.
16.
15.
14.
13.
12.
11.
10.
9.
8.
7.
6.
5.
4.
3.
2.
1.

Needle IV — Needle III — Needle II — Needle I

56-st design

Knit 2 rounds in yarn C, decreasing 4 sts evenly across first round (48 sts).

Now embroider Moomintroll and the centres of the flowers following Chart I A and Chart II. It is easier to do the embroidery when the socks are not too long and before you have closed the toe.

Check that you have 12 sts on each needle. Work the rest of the sock in yarn C.

Chart I B

Work rounds 1–39

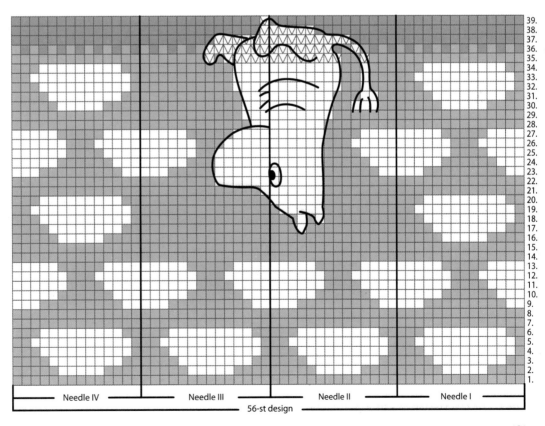

Needle IV   Needle III   Needle II   Needle I

56-st design

HEEL

Start to work heel by knitting the sts on needle I on to needle IV (24 sts for heel flap). Leave remaining sts on needles II and III. Turn work. K2, p20, k2. Turn work and start slip stitch pattern with a garter stitch edge to reinforce heel:

Row 1 (RS): k2 *sl1 (with yarn at back of work), k1*, repeat from * to * until last 2 sts, k2. Turn work.

Row 2 (WS): k2, purl until last 2 sts, k2. Turn work.

Repeat rows 1 and 2 a total of 12 times (24 rows).

Start to decrease to turn the heel:

Continue in the same slip stitch pattern as before to reinforce heel. Starting with a RS row, work in pattern until there are 9 sts left on LH needle, skpo and turn work.

Sl1 purlwise, purl 6 sts on WS until there are 9 sts left on LH needle, p2tog and turn work. **Note:** there is no garter stitch at the edges now that the rows have become shorter.

Sl1 knitwise, work in pattern until there are 8 sts left on LH needle, skpo and turn work.

Continue as set working back and forth, i.e. always slip the first st of the row and skpo at the end of a RS row and p2tog at the end of a WS row. The number of sts at the sides will always decrease by 1, always leaving 8 sts in the centre. When you run out of side sts, k4 on RS. This point (centre back) is now the start of the round.

FOOT

Knit 4 sts on LH needle from heel (needle I). Using a spare needle, pick up 12 sts from LH edge of heel flap + 1 st between heel flap and needle II. Knit picked up sts onto needle I, turning sts knitwise. Knit sts on needle II and needle III. Using the needle with 4 sts on it, pick up 12 sts from RH edge of heel flap + 1 st between heel flap and needle III. Knit picked up sts and 4 sts from heel on to needle IV, turning picked up sts knitwise. You now have 58 sts.

Continue in stocking (stockinette) stitch, decreasing for gusset as follows: k2tog at end of needle I and skpo at beginning of needle IV. Work these decreases on every alt round until there are 48 sts left.

Work in stocking (stockinette) stitch until the foot of the sock measures approximately 17cm (6¾in) or covers the wearer's little toe.

Continue in stocking (stockinette) stitch and start to decrease to work barn toe:

Needle I and needle III: knit to last 3 sts, k2tog, k1.

Needle II and needle IV: skpo, knit to end.

Decrease as set on every alt round until there are 28 sts left and then work decreases on every round until there are 8 sts left. Break yarn and thread through remaining sts.

SECOND SOCK

Work the other sock in the same way but following Chart I B for the leg.

FINISHING

Weave in ends. Carefully wet socks, place on a flat surface and block to measurements. Leave to dry. Steam block lightly if necessary.

'...The warmth made them sleepy and didn't encourage thinking, so they lay on their backs on the clouds and looked up at the spring sky where the larks were singing.'

Finn Family Moomintroll

FUN IN THE SNOW

Stinky has gone skiing and has found Moomintroll swimming in a hole in the ice. The waves and the winter sky, covered in snowflakes, are worked in traditional Fair Isle. The Moomin characters are embroidered afterwards in duplicate stitch.

DESIGNER Sonja Nykänen

SIZE UK 3½/4 (Europe 36/37, US Women's 6/6½, US Men's 4/5)

YARN

1 ball each of Novita Muumitalo (Moomin House) DK (8-ply/light worsted) yarn in Moomintroll 007 (A) and Snork 152 (B), and small amounts of Stinky 099 (C) and Fillyjonk 599 (D) or other orange yarn for the embroidery; 100g/3½oz/225m/246yd

AMOUNT USED

100g (3½oz) of yarns A and B and 25g (1oz) of yarns C and D

KNITTING NEEDLES

3mm (UK 11, US 2/3) double-pointed needles or size to obtain correct tension (gauge)

TECHNIQUES

Mock cable in the round:
Follow chart and instructions.

Stocking (stockinette) stitch in the round:
Knit all rounds.

Fair Isle in the round:
Work in stocking (stockinette) stitch following chart and instructions. Catch in any floats longer than 3 sts by twisting the yarns around each other on the wrong side. Vary where you catch your floats in the design so they don't land in the same place on consecutive rounds.

TENSION (GAUGE) 25 sts in Fair Isle = 10cm (4in)

NOTE

The socks are worked top down from cuff to toe. Stinky and Moomintroll are embroidered on top in duplicate stitch and backstitch afterwards. Divide yarn into two strands to sew the outline around Moomintroll.

Chart I

= knit

= purl

= slip 3 stitches on to right-hand needle, pass the rightmost stitch over the other 2 stitches, slip the other 2 stitches back on to the left-hand needle and knit 1, yarn over, knit 1

5-st pattern repeat

LEG

Cast on 60 sts in yarn A and divide evenly between four needles with 15 sts on each needle. The start of the round is between needle I and needle IV at the back of the sock.

Join, being careful not to twist, and start working mock cable pattern in the round from round 1 of Chart I repeating the 5-st pattern 12 times. Work all 5 rounds of chart twice and then work rounds 1–4 of chart (14 rounds). Then knit 1 round.

Change to yarn B and knit 1 round. Now start Fair Isle pattern from round 1 of Chart II, repeating the 4-st pattern to the end of the round. Work all 4 rounds of chart seven times and then work rounds 1–3 of chart (31 rounds).

Knit 9 rounds in stocking (stockinette) stitch in yarn A, decreasing 4 sts evenly across round 3 (56 sts.)

Now embroider Stinky on the front of the leg in duplicate stitch following Chart III. It is easier to do the embroidery when the socks are not too long and before you have closed the toe.

Start the Fair Isle pattern from round 1 of Chart IV, repeating the 8 st pattern seven times. Then work rounds 2–7 of chart. Break off yarn B.

Chart II

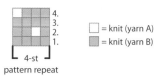

= knit (yarn A)

= knit (yarn B)

4-st pattern repeat

HEEL

Work heel in yarn A.

Start to work heel by knitting the sts on needle I on to needle IV (28 sts for heel flap). Leave remaining sts on needles II and III. Turn work. K2, p24, k2. Turn work and start slip stitch pattern with a garter stitch edge to reinforce heel:

Row 1 (RS): k2 *sl1 (with yarn at back of work), k1*, repeat from * to * until last 2 sts, k2. Turn work.

Row 2 (WS): k2, purl until last 2 sts, k2. Turn work.

Repeat rows 1 and 2 a total of 14 times (28 rows).

Start to decrease to turn the heel. Continue in the same slip stitch pattern as before to reinforce heel. Starting with a RS row, work in pattern until there are 10 sts left on LH needle, skpo and turn work.

Sl1 purlwise and purl 8 sts on WS until 10 sts remain on LH needle. P2tog and turn work. **Note:** there is no garter stitch at the edges now that the rows have become shorter.

Chart III

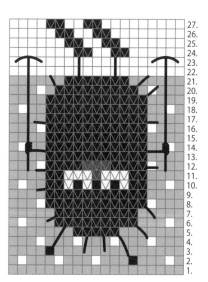

Chart IV

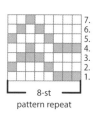

8-st pattern repeat

 = embroider sts in duplicate stitch in yarn C

= embroider sts in duplicate stitch in yarn D

= embroider sts in duplicate stitch in yarn A

= embroider in backstitch/stem stitch in yarn C

Sl1 knitwise, work in pattern until there are 9 sts left on LH needle, skpo and turn work.

Continue as set working back and forth, i.e. always slip the first st of the row and skpo at the end of a RS row and p2tog at the end of a WS row. The number of sts at the sides will decrease by 1 each time, always leaving 10 sts in the centre. When you run out of side sts at the end of a WS row, k5 on RS. This point (centre back) is now the start of the round.

FOOT
Knit 5 sts on LH needle from heel (needle I). Using a spare needle, pick up 14 sts from LH edge of heel flap + 1 st between heel flap and needle II. Knit picked up sts on to needle I, turning sts knitwise. Knit sts on needle II and needle III. Using the needle with 5 sts on it, pick up 14 sts from RH edge of heel flap + 1 st between heel flap and needle III. Knit picked up sts and 5 sts from heel on to needle IV, turning picked up sts knitwise. You now have 68 sts.

Continue in stocking (stockinette) stitch, decreasing for gusset as follows: k2tog at end of needle I and skpo at beginning of needle IV. Work this decrease on every alt round until there are 56 sts left.

Start the Fair Isle pattern from round 1 of Chart V, repeating the 8 st pattern seven times. Then work rounds 2–6 of chart.

Work 15 rounds in stocking (stockinette) stitch in yarn B.

Start working Fair Isle design from round 1 of Chart VI: repeat the 6-st pattern nine times and finally knit the 2 sts at the left side. Then work round 2 of chart.

Embroider Moomintroll in duplicate stitch in the centre on top of the foot as shown in Chart VII. It is easier to do the embroidery before you have closed the toe of the sock.

Work approximately 3cm (1¼in) in stocking (stockinette) stitch in yarn A or until the foot of the sock covers the wearer's little toe.

Continue in stocking (stockinette) stitch and start to decrease to work a barn toe:

Needle I and needle III: work to last 3 sts, k2tog, k1.

Needle II and needle IV: k1, skpo, work to end.

Decrease as set on every alt round until there are 32 sts left and then work decreases on every round until there are 8 sts left. Break yarn and thread through remaining sts.

SECOND SOCK
Work the other sock in the same way with the embroidered characters facing in the other direction.

FINISHING
Weave in ends. Carefully wet socks, place on a flat surface and block to measurements. Leave to dry. Steam gently under a cloth if necessary.

Chart V

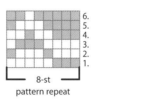

8-st pattern repeat

Chart VI

6-st pattern repeat

Chart VII

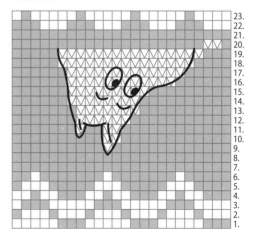

◹ = embroider sts in duplicate stitch in yarn A

◪ = embroider in backstitch in yarn C

SLEEPY SNORKMAIDEN

These charming Snorkmaiden socks start with a two-stitch cable rib. The white hearts and Snorkmaiden are worked in traditional Fair Isle. The little details are embroidered once the sock is complete. Short socks knit up quickly and fit comfortably too.

DESIGNER Sonja Nykänen

SIZE UK 5/6 (Europe 38/39, US Women's 7½/8½, US Men's 6/7)

YARN

1 ball each of Novita Muumitalo (Moomin House) DK (8-ply/light worsted) yarn in Snorkmaiden 507 (A) and Moomintroll 007 (B), and small amounts of Miffle 229 (C) and Stinky 099 (D) for the embroidery; 100g/3½oz/225m/246yd

AMOUNT USED

100g (3½oz) of yarn A, 50g (1¾oz) of yarn B and 25g (1oz) of yarns C and D

KNITTING NEEDLES

3mm (UK 11, US 2/3) double-pointed needles or size to obtain correct tension (gauge)

Cable needle

TECHNIQUES

Cable in the round:
Follow chart and instructions.

Stocking (stockinette) stitch in the round:
Knit all rounds.

Fair Isle in the round:
Work in stocking (stockinette) stitch following chart and instructions. Catch in any floats longer than 4 sts by twisting the yarns around each other at the back of the work. Vary where you catch your floats in the design so they don't land in the same place on consecutive rounds.

TENSION (GAUGE) 26 sts in Fair Isle = 10cm (4in)

NOTE

The socks are worked top down from cuff to toe. Snorkmaiden's outline and hair are embroidered afterwards in backstitch and duplicate stitch.

Chart I

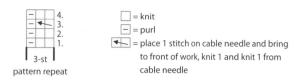

□ = knit
− = purl
⬛ = place 1 stitch on cable needle and bring to front of work, knit 1 and knit 1 from cable needle

3-st
pattern repeat

LEG

Cast on 60 sts in yarn A and divide evenly between four needles with 15 sts on each needle. The start of the round is between needle I and needle IV at the back of the sock.

Join, being careful not to twist, and start working cable pattern in the round starting at round 1 of Chart I and repeating the 3-st pattern to the end of the round. Work rows 2–4 of chart and then repeat rows 3 and 4 until leg measures approximately 9cm (3½in).

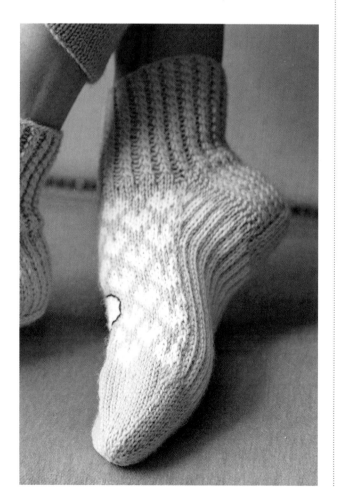

HEEL

Start to work heel by knitting the sts on needle I on to needle IV (30 sts for heel flap). Leave remaining sts on needles II and III. Turn work. K2, p26, k2. Turn work and start slip stitch pattern with a garter stitch edge to reinforce heel:

Row 1 (RS): k2 *sl1 (with yarn at back of work), k1*, repeat from * to * until last 2 sts, k2. Turn work.

Row 2 (WS): k2, purl until last 2 sts, k2. Turn work.

Repeat rows 1 and 2 a total of 15 times (30 rows).

Start to decrease to turn the heel:

Continue in the same slip stitch pattern as before to reinforce heel. Starting with a RS row, work in pattern until there are 11 sts left on LH needle, skpo and turn work.

Sl1 purlwise and purl 8 sts on WS until there are 11 sts left on LH needle. P2tog and turn work. **Note:** there is no garter stitch at the edges now that the rows have become shorter.

Sl1 knitwise, work in pattern until there are 10 sts left on LH needle, skpo and turn work.

Continue as set working back and forth, i.e. always slip the first st of the row and skpo at the end of a RS row and p2tog at the end of a WS row. The number of sts at the sides will decrease by 1 each time, always leaving 10 sts in the centre. When you run out of side sts at the end of a WS row, k5 on RS. This point is now the start of the round.

FOOT

Knit 5 sts on LH needle from heel (needle I). Using a spare needle, pick up 15 sts from LH edge of heel flap + 1 st between heel flap and needle II. Knit picked up sts on to needle I, turning sts knitwise. Knit sts on needle II and needle III. Using the needle with 5 sts on it, pick up 15 sts from RH edge of heel flap + 1 st between heel flap and needle III. Knit picked up sts and 5 sts from heel on to needle IV, turning picked up sts knitwise. You now have 72 sts and have worked the first round of Chart II A.

Work rounds 2–40 of Chart II A. Work gusset decreases following chart: at the end of needle 1 k2tog and skpo at the beginning of needle IV. Repeat decreases on every alt round until there are 60 sts left. Then continue working to the end of Chart II A.

Note: first work the sts marked in yellow in yarn B and then embroider in duplicate stitch with yarn C once you have worked all the rounds of Chart II A. Divide yarn D into two strands and embroider the outline around Snorkmaiden in backstitch.

Break off yarn B and continue in yarn A. If necessary, work additional rounds in stocking (stockinette) stitch in yarn A until the foot of the sock covers the wearer's little toe.

Knit 1 round, decreasing 4 sts evenly across round. Then start to decrease to work a star toe: k2tog at the beginning of each needle and at the middle of each needle. You will have decreased 8 sts and now have 48 sts. Work 4 rounds without decreasing and then repeat the decrease round (40 sts). Work 3 rounds without decreasing and then repeat the decrease round (32 sts).

= knit (yarn A)
= knit (yarn B)
= knit 2 together (yarn A)
= slip 1 stitch knitwise, knit 1 in yarn A and pass the slipped stitch over the knitted stitch
= embroider sts in duplicate stitch in yarn C
= embroider in backstitch in yarn D

Chart II A

Work rounds 1–40

Needle IV   Needle III   Needle II   Needle I

Continue decreasing in this way, i.e. working one fewer rounds between decrease rounds each time. When there are 16 sts left, work k2tog for the whole round (8 sts). Break yarn and thread through remaining stitches. Pull tight and weave in ends securely.

SECOND SOCK

Work the other sock in the same way but working the foot following Chart II B.

FINISHING

Weave in ends. Carefully wet socks, place on a flat surface and block to measurements. Leave to dry. Steam gently under a cloth if necessary.

= knit (yarn A)
= knit (yarn B)
= knit 2 together (yarn A)
= slip 1 stitch knitwise, knit 1 in yarn A and pass the slipped stitch over the knitted stitch
= embroider sts in duplicate stitch in yarn C
= embroider in backstitch in yarn D

Chart II B

Work rounds 1–40

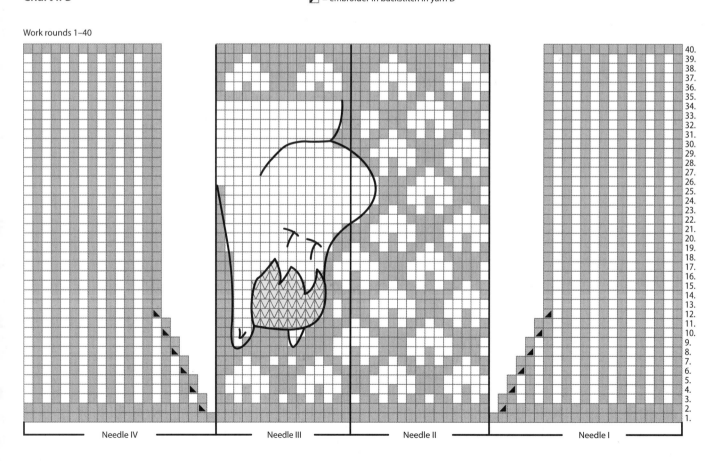

Needle IV   Needle III   Needle II   Needle I

"'...we went off to pick nine kinds of
flowers and put them under our pillow
and then our dreams came true.'"

Moominsummer Madness

MOOMINTROLL IN A HURRY

Beneath a two-colour ribbed cuff, Moomintroll hurries along a path. These children's socks are worked in traditional Fair Isle. They start at the toe and the diagonal heel is worked last.

DESIGNER Minttu Wikberg

SIZE UK Child's 13 (Europe 32, US Child's 1)

YARN
1 ball each of Novita Muumitalo (Moomin House) DK (8-ply/light worsted) yarn in Moomintroll 007 (A) and Snork 152 (B), and a small amount of Fillyjonk 599 (C); 100g/3½oz/225m/246yd

AMOUNT USED
50g (1¾oz) of yarns A and B and 25g (1oz) of yarn C

KNITTING NEEDLES
3mm (UK 11, US 2/3) double-pointed needles or size to obtain correct tension (gauge)

TECHNIQUES

Two-colour rib in the round:
knit 1 in yarn B, purl 1 in yarn A, repeat from * to *.

Stocking (stockinette) stitch in the round:
Knit all rounds.

Fair Isle in the round:
Work in stocking (stockinette) stitch following chart and instructions. Catch in any floats longer than 4 sts by twisting the yarns around each other at the back of the work. Vary where you catch your floats in the design so they don't land in the same place on consecutive rounds.

TENSION (GAUGE) 25 sts in Fair Isle = 10cm (4in)

NOTE
The socks are worked bottom up from the toe to the cuff.

FOOT

Cast on 8 sts in yarn C. Working back and forth, purl 1 row and knit 1 row. Using the same strand of yarn, pick up 8 sts from the cast-on edge (16 sts). Divide sts between four needles, 4 sts on each needle. Place different stitch markers at each side so you can tell which marks the start of the round. The start of the round is between needle I and needle IV at the side of the sock.

Work in stocking (stockinette) stitch in the round from round 2 of chart, increasing at the same time: increase 1 st at beginning of needle I and needle III and increase 1 st at the end of needle II and needle IV at the stitch markers. Increase by lifting the strand of yarn between the sts on to the needle and knitting it through the back loop. **Note:** lift the strand of yarn between the sts on to the LH needle from the front at the beginning of needles I and III and from the back at the end of needles II and IV. Then work rounds 3–15 of chart, starting the Fair Isle pattern from round 3 and continue increasing as shown. After the increases, you will have 48 sts, 12 on each needle.

Continue in Fair Isle following chart from round 16 onwards until sock measures about 11cm (4¼in) from the toe.

Mark the position of the inserted heel:

Work sts on needles I and II normally following chart. Work all sts on needles III and IV in a contrasting yarn. Break off contrasting yarn. Work sts in contrasting yarn on needles III and IV again following chart.

LEG

Continue in Fair Isle to end of chart. Then work 3cm (1¼in) in two-colour rib. Cast/bind off in rib either in one colour or two colours.

HEEL

Carefully remove contrasting yarn and using yarn B pick up 24 sts from above and below the hole and 2 additional sts from each side of the hole (52 sts). Place stitch markers at both edges, between the added sts. Divide sts evenly between four needles. The start of the round will be at the stitch marker at one side.

Work 1 round in stocking (stockinette) stitch in the round.

Start to decrease to turn heel:

Needle I and needle III: k1, k2tog through back loops, work to end.

Needle II and needle IV: work to last 3 sts, k2tog, k1.

Decrease as set on every alt round three more times and then on every round five times (16 sts).

Divide remaining sts evenly between two needles with 8 sts for the heel on the upper and lower needle. Graft sts together. There are instructions and videos available online showing how to graft (sometimes called Kitchener stitch).

SECOND SOCK

Work other sock in the same way.

FINISHING

Weave in ends. Carefully wet socks, place on a flat surface and block to measurements. Leave to dry. Steam block lightly if necessary.

■ = knit (yarn C)
U = make 1 st by picking up the yarn between the stitches and knitting it through the back loop in yarn C
☐ = knit (yarn A)
▨ = knit (yarn B)

Chart

Work rounds 1–80

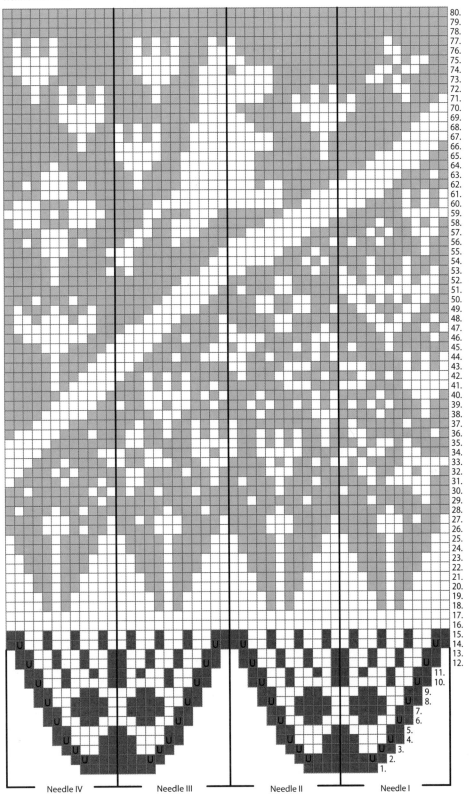

80.
79.
78.
77.
76.
75.
74.
73.
72.
71.
70.
69.
68.
67.
66.
65.
64.
63.
62.
61.
60.
59.
58.
57.
56.
55.
54.
53.
52.
51.
50.
49.
48.
47.
46.
45.
44.
43.
42.
41.
40.
39.
38.
37.
36.
35.
34.
33.
32.
31.
30.
29.
28.
27.
26.
25.
24.
23.
22.
21.
20.
19.
18.
17.
16.
15.
14.
13.
12.
11.
10.
9.
8.
7.
6.
5.
4.
3.
2.
1.

Needle IV — Needle III — Needle II — Needle I

THE HATTIFATTENERS ARE COMING

These socks show the Hattifatteners, eerie creatures that move in large groups, eagerly awaiting bolts of lightning. These creatures are easy to knit as the Fair Isle design only uses two colours in each row. The heel is worked last and is decreased in the same way as the toe. The leg is wide, making these socks a comfortable fit.

DESIGNER Minttu Wikberg

SIZE UK 5/6 (Europe 38/39, US Women's 7½/8½, US Men's 6/7)

YARN
1 ball each of Novita Muumitalo (Moomin House) DK (8-ply/light worsted) yarn in The Groke 176 (A), Moomintroll 007 (B) and Hemulen 720 (C), and a small amount of The Groke 176 (A) for the embroidery; 100g/3½oz/225m/246yd

AMOUNT USED
100g (3½oz) of yarns A, B and C

KNITTING NEEDLES
3mm (UK 11, US 2/3) double-pointed needles or size to obtain correct tension (gauge)

TECHNIQUES

Twisted rib in the round:
knit 1 through back loop, purl 1, repeat from * to *.

Stocking (stockinette) stitch in the round:
Knit all rounds.

Fair Isle in the round:
Work in stocking (stockinette) stitch following chart and instructions. Catch in any floats longer than 4 sts by twisting the yarns around each other at the back of the work. Vary where you catch your floats in the design so they don't land in the same place on consecutive rounds.

TENSION (GAUGE) 25 sts in Fair Isle = 10cm (4in)

NOTE
The socks are worked top down from cuff to toe with the heel inserted at the end. Embroider the Hattifatteners' eyes in duplicate stitch as you go along or once the sock is finished.

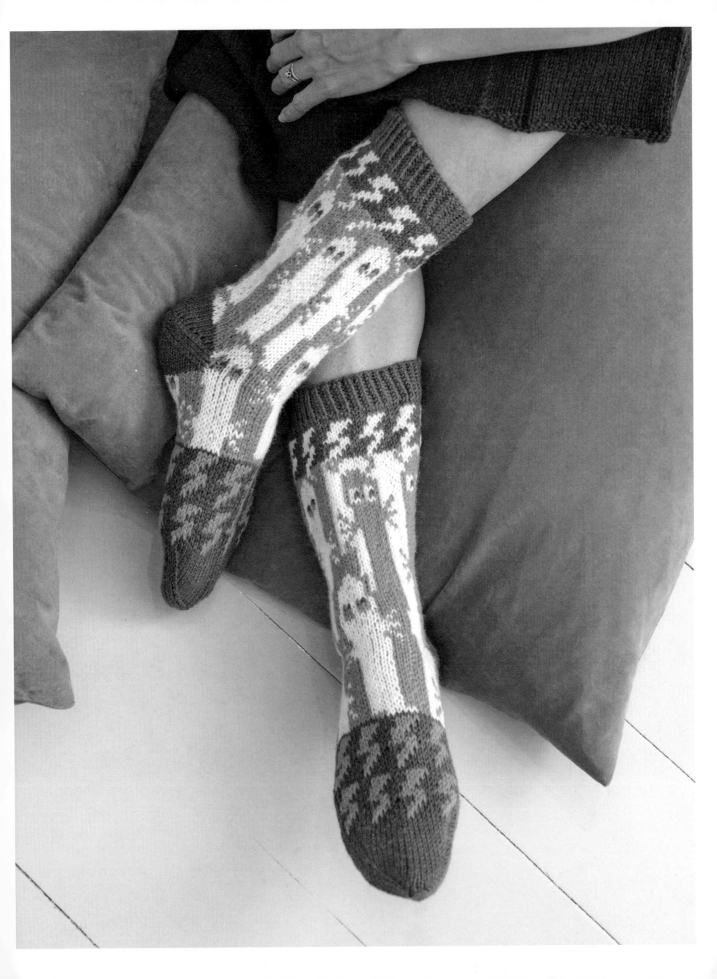

LEG AND FOOT

Cast on 70 sts in yarn A and divide between four needles as follows: 21 sts on needles I and IV and 14 sts on needles II and III. The start of the round is between needle I and needle IV at the back of the sock.

Join, being careful not to twist, and work 3cm (1¼in) in twisted rib in the round. Then knit 1 round.

Start Fair Isle pattern working round 1 of Chart I. Then work rounds 2–51 of chart. Decrease at places marked on chart. **Note:** embroider the Hattifatteners' eyes in duplicate stitch as you go along or once the sock is finished.

Work round 52 of Chart I on needles I–III and then mark the place for the heel:

Work sts on needle IV and needle I in a contrasting yarn. Break off contrasting yarn. Work sts in contrasting yarn again, on needle IV work to the end of Chart I and on needle I start round 1 of Chart II.

Work to the end of round 1 on Chart II. You now have 56 sts. Work rounds 2–16 of Chart II.

■ = knit (yarn A)
□ = knit (yarn B)
▨ = knit (yarn C)
◢ = knit 2 together (yarn C)
◣ = knit 2 together through back loops (yarn C)
▼ = embroider sts in duplicate stitch in yarn A
— = position of inserted heel

Chart I

Work rounds 1–52

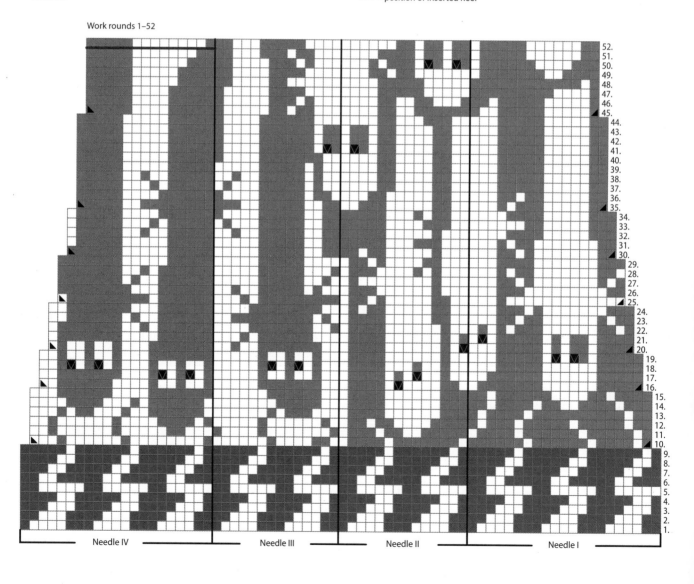

Needle IV — Needle III — Needle II — Needle I

Continue working Fair Isle pattern from round 1 of Chart III, repeating the 7-st pattern eight times. Work rounds 2–10 of chart, then repeat rounds 1–10 until the foot of the sock measures about 14cm (5½in) from the contrasting yarn or until the foot covers the wearer's little toe. Then continue in yarn A and start to decrease for the toe. **Note:** if you are in the middle of a bolt of lightning, complete it as you work the toe decreases. Then work to the end of the toe in yarn A.

Decrease for barn toe as follows:

Needle I and needle III: work to last 3 sts, k2tog, k1.

Needle II and needle IV: k1, skpo, work to end.

Decrease as set on every alt round until there are 24 sts left and then work decreases on every round until there are 8 sts left. Break yarn and thread through remaining sts.

HEEL

Carefully remove contrasting yarn and using yarn A pick up 28 sts from above and below the hole and 2 additional sts from each side of the hole (60 sts). Place stitch markers at both edges, between the added sts. Divide sts evenly between four needles. The start of the round will be at the stitch marker at one side.

Work 1 round in stocking (stockinette) stitch in the round.

Start to decrease to work heel:

Needle I and needle III: k1, k2tog through back loops, work to end.

Chart III

Repeat rounds 1–10

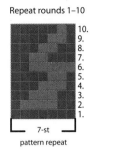

= knit (yarn A)
= knit (yarn C)

7-st
pattern repeat

Needle II and needle IV: work to last 3 sts, k2tog, k1.

Decrease as set on every alt round four more times and then on every round five times (20 sts).

Divide remaining sts evenly between two needles with 10 sts for the heel on the upper and lower needle. Graft sts together. There are instructions and videos available online showing how to graft (sometimes called Kitchener stitch).

SECOND SOCK

Work other sock in the same way.

FINISHING

Weave in ends. Carefully wet socks, place on a flat surface and block to measurements. Leave to dry. Steam block lightly if necessary.

= knit (yarn B)
= knit (yarn C)
= embroider sts in duplicate stitch in yarn A

Chart II

Work rounds 1–16

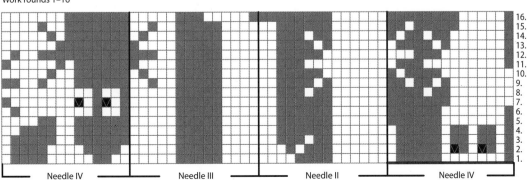

X MARKS THE SPOT

In these socks designed by Minttu Wikberg, Moominpappa is peacefully sailing towards the lighthouse. A misty sky and soaring seagulls add to the maritime atmosphere. The fun striped pattern from ankle to toe is worked easily thanks to self-striping yarn.

DESIGNER Minttu Wikberg

SIZE UK 8 (Europe 42, US Women's 10½, US Men's 9)

YARN

1 ball each of Novita Muumitalo (Moomin House) DK (8-ply/light worsted) yarn in Snorkmaiden 507 (A) and The Groke 176 (B); 100g/3½oz/225m/246yd

1 ball of Novita Muumihahmot (Moomin Characters) DK (8-ply/light worsted) yarn in Moominpappa 821 (C); 100g/3½oz/225m/246yd

AMOUNT USED

50g (1¾oz) of yarns A and B and 100g (3½oz) of yarn C

KNITTING NEEDLES

3mm (UK 11, US 2/3) double-pointed needles or size to obtain correct tension (gauge)

TECHNIQUES

Rib in the round:
knit 2, purl 2, repeat from * to *.

Stocking (stockinette) stitch in the round:
Knit all rounds.

Fair Isle in the round:
Work in stocking (stockinette) stitch following chart and instructions. Catch in any floats longer than 4 sts by twisting the yarns around each other at the back of the work. Vary where you catch your floats in the design so they don't land in the same place on consecutive rounds.

TENSION (GAUGE) 25 sts = 10cm (4in)

NOTE

The socks are worked top down from cuff to toe.

LEG

Cast on 60 sts in yarn A and divide between four needles as follows: 16 sts on needles I and III and 14 sts on needles II and IV. The start of the round is between needle I and needle IV at the back of the sock.

Join, being careful not to twist, and work 4cm (1½in) in rib in the round. Then knit 8 rounds in stocking (stockinette) stitch in the round, increasing 1 st on needles II and IV on the last round (62 sts).

Start the Fair Isle pattern, working round 1 of Chart I A across all 62 sts. Then work rounds 2–32 of chart. Break off yarn A.

Join yarn C (self-striping yarn) and work rounds 33 and 34 of chart. **Note:** start yarn C from the light blue colour. Work last round of chart, decreasing 1 st on needles I and III (60 sts). Break off yarn B and work the rest of the sock in yarn C.

HEEL

Start to work heel by knitting the sts on needle I on to needle IV (30 sts for heel flap). Leave remaining sts on needles II and III. Turn work and start slip stitch pattern to reinforce heel:

Row 1 (WS): sl1 (with yarn at back of work), purl to end of row. Turn work.

Row 2 (RS): *sl1 (with yarn at back of work), k1*, repeat from * to * to end of row. Turn work.

Repeat rows 1 and 2 a total of 15 times and then knit 1 row (31 rows).

Start to decrease to turn the heel:

Continue in the same slip stitch pattern as before to reinforce heel. Starting with a RS row, work in pattern until there are 11 sts left on LH needle, skpo and turn work.

Sl1 purlwise and purl 8 sts on WS until there are 11 sts left on LH needle. P2tog and turn work.

Sl1 knitwise, work in pattern until there are 10 sts left on LH needle, skpo and turn work.

☐ = knit (yarn A)
■ = knit (yarn B)
☐ = knit (yarn C)

Chart I A   Work rounds 1–35

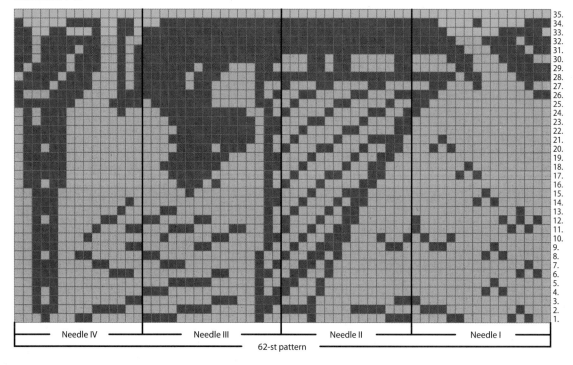

Needle IV ⸺ Needle III ⸺ Needle II ⸺ Needle I

62-st pattern

35.
34.
33.
32.
31.
30.
29.
28.
27.
26.
25.
24.
23.
22.
21.
20.
19.
18.
17.
16.
15.
14.
13.
12.
11.
10.
9.
8.
7.
6.
5.
4.
3.
2.
1.

Continue as set working back and forth, i.e. always slip the first st of the row and skpo at the end of a RS row and p2tog at the end of a WS row. The number of sts at the sides will decrease by 1 each time, always leaving 10 sts in the centre. When you run out of side sts at the end of a WS row, k5 on RS. This point (centre back) is now the start of the round.

FOOT

Knit 5 sts on LH needle from heel (needle I). Using a spare needle, pick up 15 sts from LH edge of heel flap + 1 st between heel flap and needle II. Knit picked up sts on to needle I, turning sts knitwise. Knit sts on needle II and needle III. Using the needle with 5 sts on it, pick up 15 sts from RH edge of heel flap + 1 st between heel flap and needle III. Knit picked up sts and 5 sts from heel on to needle IV, turning picked up sts knitwise. You now have 72 sts.

Continue in stocking (stockinette) stitch, decreasing for gusset as follows: k2tog at end of needle I and skpo at beginning of needle IV. Work this decrease on every alt round until there are 60 sts left, 15 on each needle.

Work in stocking (stockinette) stitch until the foot of the sock measures approximately 21cm (8¼in) or covers the wearer's little toe. Then k2tog at the end of each needle (56 sts).

Continue in stocking (stockinette) stitch and start to decrease to work a star toe: k2tog in the middle and at the end of each needle. You will have decreased 8 sts and now have 48 sts. Work 5 rounds without decreasing and then repeat the decrease round (40 sts). Work 4 rounds without decreasing and then repeat the decrease round (32 sts).

Continue decreasing in this way, i.e. working one fewer round between decrease rounds each time. When there are 8 sts left, break off yarn and thread through remaining stitches. Pull tight and weave in ends securely.

SECOND SOCK

Work the other sock in the same way but following Chart I B for the leg.

FINISHING

Weave in ends. Carefully wet socks, place on a flat surface and block to measurements. Leave to dry. Steam block lightly if necessary.

Chart I B Work rounds 1–35

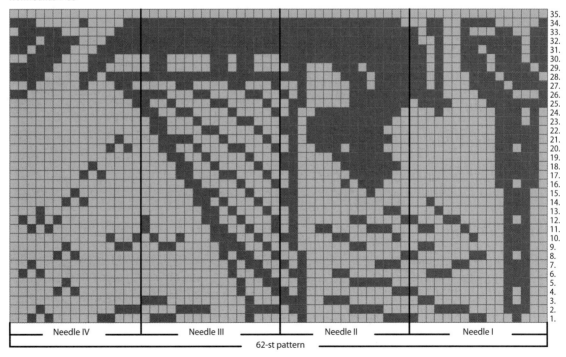

SNUFKIN GOES FISHING

These socks, inspired by Snufkin the wanderer, begin with a traditional ribbed cuff. The two-colour sections, with Snufkin on the calf and a shoal of fish on the foot are worked using a traditional Fair Isle technique. The socks have a classic heel and a barn toe.

DESIGNER Sonja Nykänen

SIZE UK 4/5 (Europe 37/38, US Women's 6½/7½, US Men's 5/6)

YARN

1 ball each of Novita Muumitalo (Moomin House) DK (8-ply/light worsted) yarn in Snufkin 381 (A) and Moomintroll 007 (B); 100g/3½oz/225m/246yd

AMOUNT USED

100g (3½oz) of yarns A and B

KNITTING NEEDLES

3mm (UK 11, US 2/3) double-pointed needles or size to obtain correct tension (gauge)

TECHNIQUES

Rib in the round:
knit 2, purl 2, repeat from * to *.

Stocking (stockinette) stitch in the round:
Knit all rounds.

Fair Isle in the round:
Work in stocking (stockinette) stitch following chart and instructions. In Fair Isle sections, catch in any floats longer than 3 sts by twisting the yarns around each other at the back of the work. Vary where you catch your floats in the design so they don't land in the same place on consecutive rounds.

TENSION (GAUGE) 25 sts in Fair Isle = 10cm (4in)

NOTE
The socks are worked top down from cuff to toe.

LEG

Cast on 60 sts in yarn B and divide between four needles as follows: 16 sts on needles I and III and 14 sts on needles II and IV. The start of the round is between needle I and needle IV at the back of the sock.

Join, being careful not to twist, and work 6cm (2¼in) in rib in the round. Knit 1 round, increasing 4 sts evenly across round (64 sts). Divide sts evenly with 16 sts on each needle.

Start the Fair Isle pattern following round 1 of Chart I and repeating the 16-st pattern four times. Then work rounds 2–36 of chart.

Continue in yarn A. Knit 1 round, decreasing 4 sts evenly across round (60 sts).

Work approximately 5cm (2in) in rib in the round. On last round of rib decrease 4 sts evenly across round (56 sts).

Chart I

Work rounds 1–36

16-st pattern repeat

Chart II

Work rounds 1–19

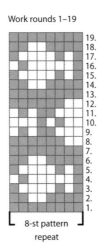

8-st pattern repeat

☐ = knit (yarn B)
▩ = knit (yarn A)

HEEL

Start to work heel by knitting the sts on needle I on to needle IV (28 sts for heel flap). Leave remaining sts on needles II and III. Turn work. K2, p24, k2. Turn work and start slip stitch pattern with a garter stitch edge to reinforce heel:

Row 1 (RS): k2 *sl1 (with yarn at back of work), k1*, repeat from * to * until last 2 sts, k2. Turn work.

Row 2 (WS): k2, purl until last 2 sts, k2. Turn work.

Repeat rows 1 and 2 a total of 14 times (28 rows).

Start to decrease to turn the heel. Continue in the same slip stitch pattern as before to reinforce heel. Starting with a RS row, work in pattern until there are 10 sts left on LH needle, skpo and turn work.

Sl1 purlwise and purl 8 sts on WS until there are 10 sts left on LH needle. P2tog and turn work. **Note:** you won't be working garter stitch at the edges any more as the rows have got shorter.

Starting with a RS row, sl1 knitwise, work in pattern until there are 9 sts left on LH needle, skpo and turn work.

Continue as set working back and forth, i.e. always slip the first st of the row and skpo at the end of a RS row and p2tog at the end of a WS row. The number of sts at the sides will decrease by 1 each time, always leaving 10 sts in the centre. When you run out of side sts at the end of a WS row, k5 on RS. This point (centre back) is now the start of the round.

FOOT

Knit 5 sts on LH needle from heel (needle I). Using a spare needle, pick up 14 sts from LH edge of heel flap + 1 st between heel flap and needle II. Knit picked up sts on to needle I, turning sts knitwise. Knit sts on needle II and needle III. Using the needle with 5 sts on it, pick up 14 sts from RH edge of heel flap + 1 st between heel flap and needle III.

Knit picked up sts and 5 sts from heel on to needle IV, turning picked up sts knitwise (68 sts).

Continue in stocking (stockinette) stitch, decreasing for gusset as follows: k2tog at end of needle I and skpo at beginning of needle IV. Work this decrease on every alt round until there are 56 sts left.

Now start Fair Isle pattern from round 1 of Chart II, repeating the 8-st pattern seven times. Then work rounds 2–19 of chart.

Work approximately 3cm (1¼in) in stocking (stockinette) stitch in yarn A or until the foot of the sock covers the wearer's little toe.

Continue in stocking (stockinette) stitch and start to decrease to work a barn toe:

Needle I and needle III: work to last 3 sts, k2tog, k1.

Needle II and needle IV: k1, skpo, work to end.

Decrease as set on every alt round until there are 32 sts left and then work decreases on every round until there are 8 sts left. Break yarn and thread through remaining sts.

SECOND SOCK

Work the other sock in the same way.

FINISHING

Weave in ends. Carefully wet socks, place on a flat surface and block to measurements. Leave to dry. Steam block lightly if necessary.

ZZZZ...
TIME FOR A SNOOZE

Snorkmaiden dozing in a bed of flowers inspired Sisko Sälpäkivi to design these cute children's socks. Snorkmaiden is worked in intarsia and the details are embroidered on afterwards. The cuff of this short sock is worked in twisted rib and the heel is reinforced. The socks are then finished with a barn toe.

DESIGNER Sisko Sälpäkivi

SIZE UK Child's 11½(13:UK Adult's 2) (Europe 30(32:34), US Child's 12(13½:US Women's 4, US Men's 2½))

YARN

1 ball each of Novita Muumitalo (Moomin House) DK (8-ply/light worsted) yarn in Snork 152 (A), Snufkin 381 (B) and Moomintroll 007 (C), and small amounts in Miffle 229 (D), Fillyjonk 599 (E), Snorkmaiden 507 (F) and Stinky (G) for the embroidery; 100g/3½oz/225m/246yd

AMOUNT USED

50g (1¾oz) of yarns A, B and C for all sizes, 25g (1oz) of yarns E, F and G

KNITTING NEEDLES

3mm (UK 11, US 2/3) double-pointed needles or size to obtain correct tension (gauge)

TECHNIQUES

Twisted rib in the round:
knit 1 through back loop, purl 1, repeat from * to *.

Stocking (stockinette) stitch in the round:
Knit all rounds.

Intarsia in the round:
Knit on RS and purl on WS following instructions. Use a separate ball of wool for each section of colour and twist the different coloured yarns around each other at back of work where the two meet so as not to form holes.

TENSION (GAUGE) 25 sts in st st = 10cm (4in)

NOTE

The socks are worked top down from cuff to toe. Work Snorkmaiden and the background using intarsia in the round and embroider the details on afterwards following the instructions. Alternatively, work the leg in rows with either backstitch or lazy daisy stitch and sew a seam at the back at the end. If using this method, add 1 st at each edge to act as a seam allowance and decrease these sts before working the heel.

LEFT SOCK

Cast on 50(52:54) sts in yarn A and divide between four needles as follows: 13(13:14) sts on needle I, 12(13:13) sts on needle II, 12(13:13) sts on needle III and 13(13:14) sts on needle IV. The start of the round is between needle I and needle IV at the back of the sock.

Join, being careful not to twist, and work 2.5cm (1in) in rib and then knit 4 rounds in stocking (stockinette) stitch.

Start working intarsia in the round from round 5 of Chart I working across all 50(52:54) sts: *turn work, yarn over and purl next round of chart. At end of round purl last st of round and the yarn over from the beginning of the round together. Turn work, yarn over and knit next round of chart. Work the yarn over from the beginning of the round and the last st together using skpo*. Repeat from * to * until you have worked round 29 of chart.

Note: work decreases on round 21 of chart as follows: at beginning of round yarn over, k2tog and work to last 3 sts in round, skpo and then work the last st in the round together with the yarn over from the beginning of the round using skpo.

Then work 7 rounds in stocking (stockinette) stitch in the round in yarn B (rounds 30–36 of chart).

Once you have completed the chart, you will have 48(50:52) sts.

For smallest and largest sizes, divide sts evenly between needles, for medium size: 13+12+12+13 sts.

□ = knit (yarn A)
□ = knit (yarn C)
□ = knit (yarn D)
■ = knit (yarn B)

Chart I

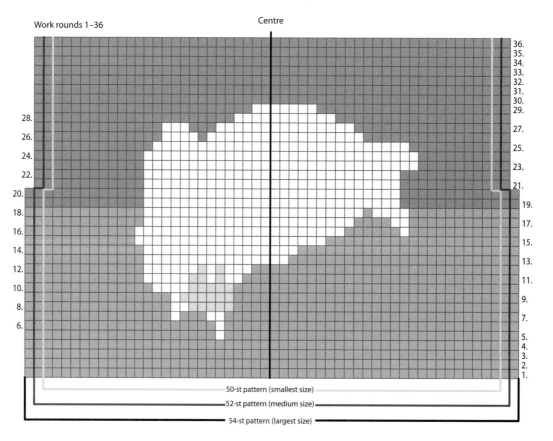

HEEL

Work heel in yarn B.

Start to work heel by knitting the sts on needle I on to needle IV. For medium size also decrease 2 sts evenly (24(24:26) sts for heel flap). Leave remaining sts on needles II and III. Turn work and start slip stitch pattern to reinforce heel:

Row 1 (WS): sl1 (with yarn at back of work), purl to end of row. Turn work.

Row 2 (RS): *sl1 (with yarn at back of work), k1*, repeat from * to * to end of row. Turn work.

Repeat rows 1 and 2 a total of 12(12:13) times and then knit 1 row (25(25:27) sts).

Start to decrease to turn the heel:

Continue in the same slip stitch pattern as before to reinforce heel. Starting with a RS row, work in pattern until there are 9(9:10) sts left on LH needle, skpo and turn work.

Sl1 purlwise and purl 6 sts on WS until there are 9(9:10) sts left on LH needle. P2tog and turn work.

Sl1 knitwise, work in pattern until there are 8(8:9) sts left on LH needle, skpo and turn work.

Continue as set working back and forth, i.e. always slip the first st of the row and skpo at the end of a RS row and p2tog at the end of a WS row. The number of sts at the sides will always decrease by 1, always leaving 8 sts in the centre. When you run out of side sts, k4 on RS. This point (centre back) is now the start of the round. Break off yarn B.

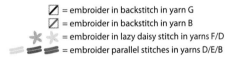

☑ = embroider in backstitch in yarn G
☑ = embroider in backstitch in yarn B
✳ ✳ = embroider in lazy daisy stitch in yarns F/D
▬ ▬ ▬ = embroider parallel stitches in yarns D/E/B

Chart II

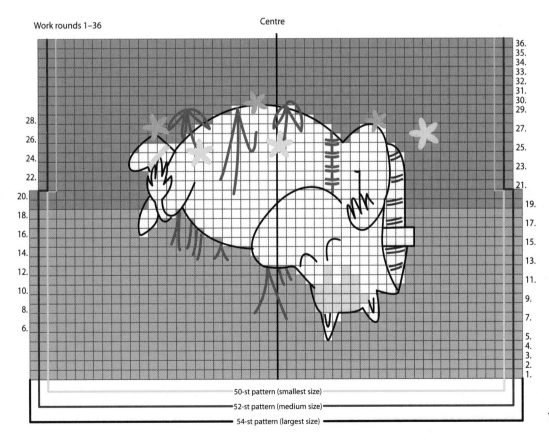

Work rounds 1–36

Centre

50-st pattern (smallest size)
52-st pattern (medium size)
54-st pattern (largest size)

FOOT

Using yarn C, knit 4 sts on LH needle from heel (needle I). Using a spare needle, pick up 12(12:13) sts from LH edge of heel flap + 1 st between heel flap and needle II.

Knit picked up sts on to needle I, turning sts knitwise. Knit sts on needle II and needle III. Using the needle with 4 sts on it, pick up 12(12:13) sts from RH edge of heel flap + 1 st between heel flap and needle III. Knit picked up sts and 4 sts from heel on to needle IV, turning picked up sts knitwise. You now have 58(58:62) sts.

Continue in stocking (stockinette) stitch, decreasing for gusset as follows: k2tog at end of needle I and skpo at beginning of needle IV. Work this decrease on every alt round until there are 48(50:52) sts left. For smallest and largest sizes, divide sts evenly between needles, for medium size: 13+12+12+13 sts.

Continue in stocking (stockinette) stitch until the foot of the sock measures approximately 15(16:17)cm / 6(6¼:6¾)in or covers the wearer's little toe.

For the medium size, knit one more round, decreasing 1 st on needles I and IV (48 sts). Divide sts evenly between needles.

Continue in stocking (stockinette) stitch using yarn B and start to decrease to work a barn toe:

Needle I and needle III: work to last 3 sts, k2tog, k1.

Needle II and needle IV: k1, skpo, work to end.

Repeat these decreases on every alt round until there are 24 sts left and then on every round until there are 8 sts left. Break yarn and thread through remaining sts.

RIGHT SOCK

Work the other sock in the same way but knit the leg with the design reversed following Chart II. The embroidery is also marked on Chart II.

FINISHING

Embroider details using Chart II to help you. Embroider the black outline around Snorkmaiden and the grass in backstitch. Embroider the flowers in lazy daisy stitch and work parallel stitches for the stripes on the pillow, Snorkmaiden's ankle bracelet and the leaves under her arm. If you like, you could also add flowers at the back of the leg.

Weave in ends. Carefully wet socks, place on a flat surface and block to measurements. Leave to dry. Steam block lightly if necessary.

'The air was sweet with
the smell of flowers.'

Finn Family Moomintroll

A SOCK FOR YOU

Personalize your own Moomin socks! At the end of the instructions you can choose your own initial and combine it with a character from Moomin Valley. Worked in the traditional Fair Isle technique, these socks knit up easily without long floats.

DESIGNER Minna Metsänen

SIZE UK 5/6 (Europe 38/39, US Women's 7½/8½, US Men's 6/7)

YARN

1 ball of Novita Muumitalo (Moomin House) DK (8-ply/light worsted) yarn in Snorkmaiden 507 (A) and a small amount of Stinky 099 (B) for the embroidery; 100g/3½oz/225m/246yd

1 ball of Novita Huviretki (Adventure) DK (8-ply/light worsted) yarn in Beach 652 (C); 50g/1¾oz/112m/122yd

AMOUNT USED

100g (3½oz) of yarn A, 50g (1¾oz) of yarn C and 25g (1oz) of yarn B.

KNITTING NEEDLES

3mm (UK 11, US 2/3) double-pointed needles or size to obtain correct tension (gauge)

TECHNIQUES

Twisted rib in the round:
knit 1 through back loop, purl 1, repeat from * to *.

Stocking (stockinette) stitch in the round:
Knit all rounds.

Fair Isle:
Work in stocking (stockinette) stitch following chart and instructions. Catch in any floats longer than 4 sts by twisting the yarns around each other at the back of the work. Vary where you catch your floats in the design so they don't land in the same place on consecutive rounds.

TENSION (GAUGE) 25 sts in Fair Isle = 10cm (4in)

NOTE

Instead of an 'N', you can use the letter of your choice from the templates on pages 162–165. Remember to read the letter charts upside down so the top of the letter is at the top of the sock. Follow the same pattern as shown for the stitches around the letters.

LEG

Cast/bind on 64 sts in yarn A and divide evenly between four needles with 16 sts on each needle. The start of the round is between needle I and needle IV at the side of the sock.

Join, being careful not to twist, and work 3cm (1¼in) in rib and then knit 2 rounds in stocking (stockinette) stitch.

Start the Fair Isle pattern, working round 1 of Chart I A across all 64 sts. Then work rounds 2–37 of chart. Break off yarn C.

Knit 2 rounds in yarn A and then knit sts on needles I and II.

HEEL

Start to work heel by knitting the sts on needle IV on to needle III and decrease 4 sts evenly (28 sts for heel flap). Leave remaining sts on needles I and II. Turn work and purl heel flap sts.

Turn work and start slip stitch pattern to reinforce heel:

Row 1 (RS): *sl1 (with yarn at back of work), k1*, repeat from * to * to end of row. Turn work.

Row 2 (WS): sl1 (with yarn at back of work), purl to end of row. Turn work.

Repeat rows 1 and 2 a total of 14 times (28 rows).

Start to decrease to turn the heel:

Continue in the same slip stitch pattern as before to reinforce heel. Starting with a RS row, work in pattern until there are 10 sts left on LH needle, skpo and turn work.

Sl1 purlwise and purl 8 sts on WS until 10 sts remain on LH needle. P2tog and turn work.

Chart I A

☐ = knit (yarn A)
■ = knit (yarn C)

Work rounds 1–37

64-st pattern

Needle IV   Needle III   Needle II   Needle I

Sl1 knitwise, work in pattern until there are 9 sts left on LH needle, skpo and turn work.

Continue as set working back and forth, i.e. always slip the first st of the row and skpo at the end of a RS row and p2tog at the end of a WS row. The number of sts at the sides will decrease by 1 each time, always leaving 10 sts in the centre. When you run out of side sts at the end of a WS row, k5 on RS. This is now the beginning of the round (between what is now needle IV and needle I).

FOOT
Knit 5 sts on LH needle from heel (this is now needle I). Using a spare needle, pick up 14 sts from LH edge of heel flap + 1 st between heel flap and needle II. Knit picked up sts on to needle I, turning sts knitwise. Knit sts on needle II and needle III. Using the needle with 5 sts on it, pick up 14 sts from RH edge of heel flap + 1 st between heel flap and needle III. Knit picked up sts and 5 sts from heel on to needle IV, turning picked up sts knitwise. You now have 72 sts.

Start Fair Isle pattern from round 1 of Chart II (overleaf): work first 16 sts on needle I following chart and work last 4 sts of needle in yarn A, work sts on needles II and III following chart, work 4 sts in yarn A at start of needle IV and then work 16 sts following chart. Continue working 'extra' sts in yarn A at end of needle I and beginning of needle IV until they have all been decreased.

Starting from round 2 of Chart II work gusset decreases as follows: k2tog at end of needle I and skpo at beginning of needle IV. Continue working chart rounds in order and repeat this decrease on every alt round until there are 64 sts left, 16 on each needle.

Chart I B

Work rounds 1–37

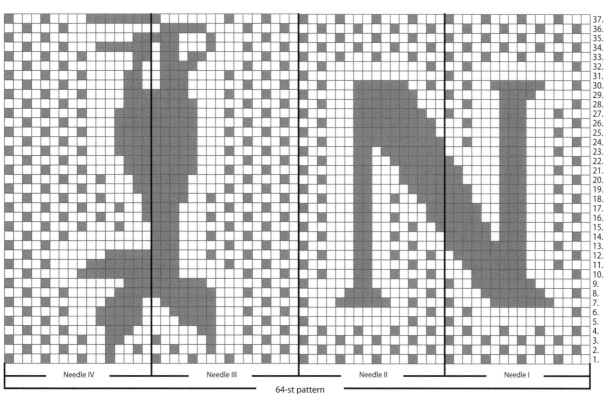

Needle IV   Needle III   Needle II   Needle I

64-st pattern

Work to end of chart and then repeat rounds 36 and 37 until foot of sock measures approximately 19cm (7½in) or covers the wearer's little toe. Break off yarn C. Knit 1 round in yarn A, decreasing 8 sts evenly across round (56 sts, 14 on each needle).

Continue in stocking (stockinette) stitch and start to decrease to work a barn toe:

Needle I and needle III: work to last 3 sts, k2tog, k1.

Needle II and needle IV: k1, skpo, work to end.

Repeat these decreases on every alt round until there are 24 sts left and then on every round until there are 8 sts left. Break yarn and thread through remaining sts.

SECOND SOCK

Work as for first sock but work Fair Isle pattern for leg following Chart I B.

FINISHING

Embroider details as shown in Chart III. Divide yarn B into two strands and embroider the outline of Sniff and other lines using short backstitches. Embroider French knots in yarn B for eyes and nose.

Weave in ends. Carefully wet socks, place on a flat surface and block to measurements. Leave to dry. Steam block lightly if necessary.

Chart II

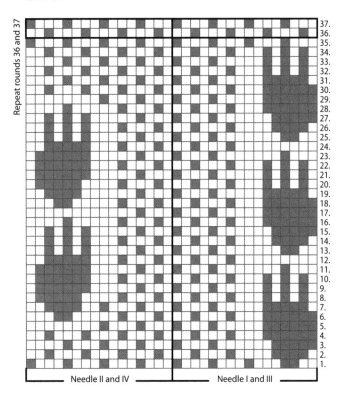

 = knit (yarn A)

▩ = knit (yarn C)

Chart III

✏ = embroider in backstitch in yarn B

⦿ = embroider a French knot in yarn B

160

"'I'm the culprit,"
squeaked Sniff. "So you
can thank me!'"

Finn Family Moomintroll

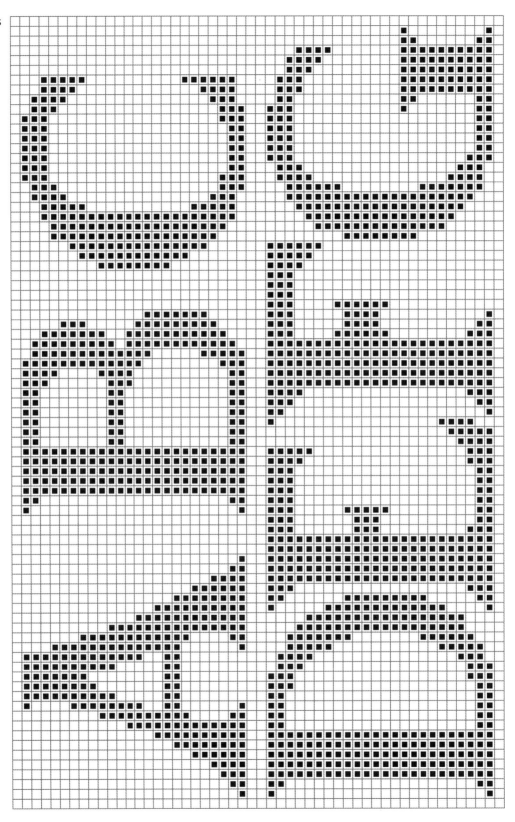

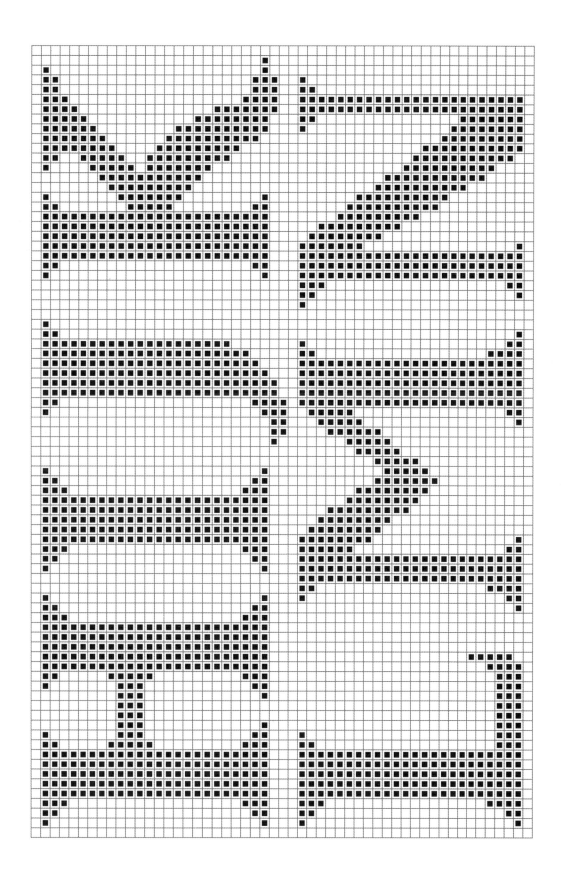

Letter templates

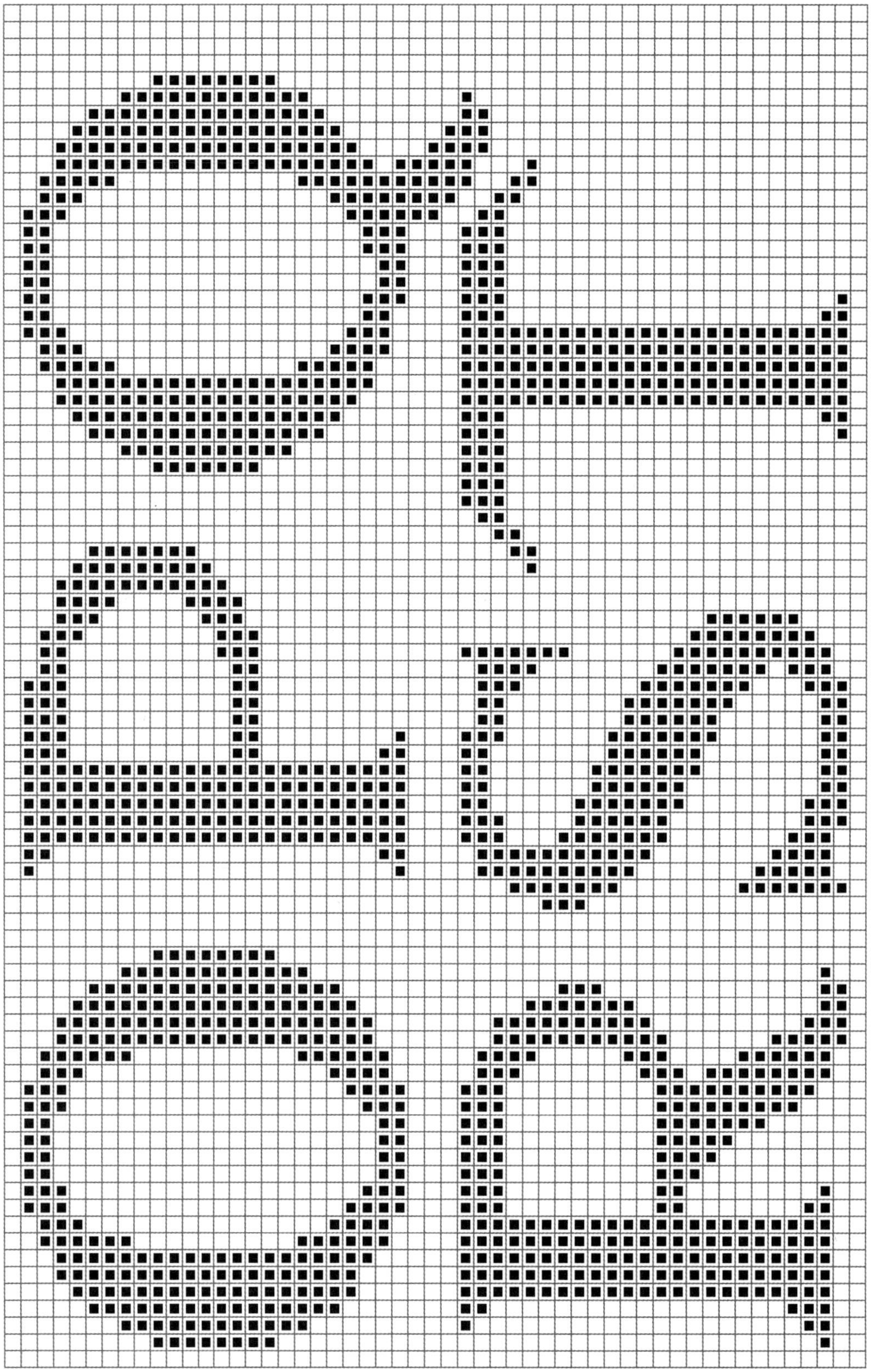

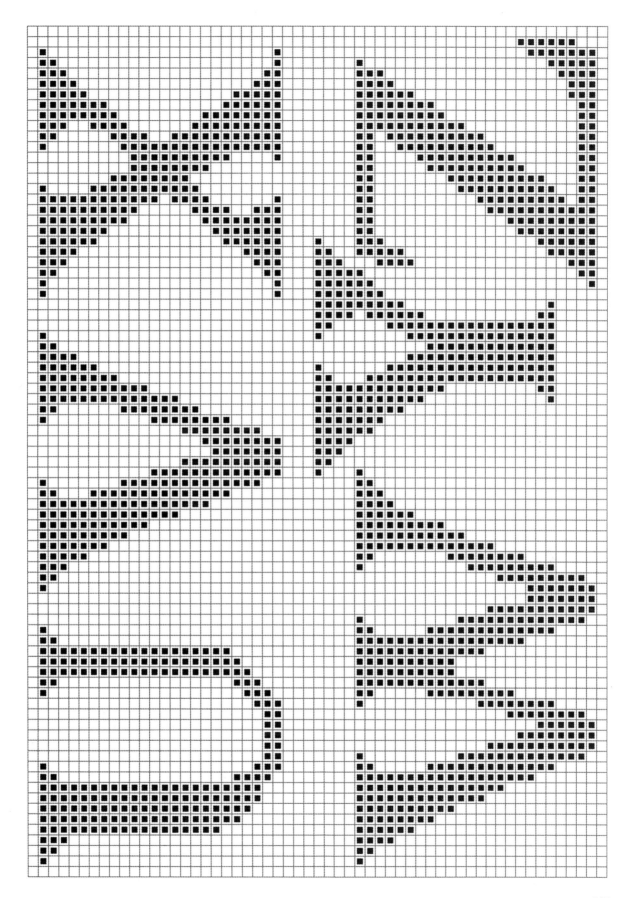

A BIG MOOMIN HUG

Moomintroll is comforted by his mother on the legs of these socks that extend halfway up the calf. The Fair Isle design on the leg is worked using the ladder back jacquard technique. The cuff is knitted in twisted rib and the heel is a traditional slip stitch reinforced heel. The length of the foot can easily be adapted to the size desired.

DESIGNER Marita Karlsson

SIZES UK 5/6(6½/7½) (Europe 38/39(40/41), US Women's 7½/8½(9/10), US Men's 6/7(7½/8½))

YARN
2 balls of Novita Muumitalo (Moomin House) DK (8-ply/light worsted) yarn in Fillyjonk 599 (A) and 1 ball in Moomintroll 007 (B); 100g/3½oz/225m/246yd

AMOUNT USED
200g (7oz) of yarn A and 100g (3½oz) of yarn B for both sizes

KNITTING NEEDLES
3mm (UK 11, US 2/3) double-pointed needles or size to obtain correct tension (gauge)

TECHNIQUES

Twisted rib in the round:
knit 1 through back loop, purl 1, repeat from * to *.

Stocking (stockinette) stitch in the round:
Knit all rounds.

Fair Isle in the round:
Work in stocking (stockinette) stitch following chart and instructions. Catch in any floats longer than 4 sts by twisting the yarns around each other at the back of the work. Vary where you catch your floats in the design so they don't land in the same place on consecutive rounds. Use the ladder back jacquard technique to catch in floats on the leg. You can find videos and instructions showing how to do this online.

TENSION (GAUGE) 29 sts in Fair Isle = 10cm (4in)

NOTE
The socks are worked top down from cuff to toe.

LEG

Cast on 80(84) sts in yarn A and divide between four needles as follows: 25(27) sts on needles I and IV and 15(15) sts on needles II and III. The start of the round is between needle I and needle IV at the back of the sock.

Join, being careful not to twist, and work 4.5cm (1¾in) in twisted rib in the round. Knit one round, decreasing 4 sts evenly across round (76(80) sts).

Start the Fair Isle pattern, working round 1 of chart across all 76(80) sts. Then work rounds 2–62(2–67) of chart. Decrease at places marked on chart. **Note:** when following the instructions for the larger size, always treat the decrease st for the smaller size as a knit st and work it in the yarn as shown by the colour of the square.

Break off yarn B and work the rest of the sock in yarn A. Work 4cm (1½in) in stocking (stockinette) stitch.

Divide sts evenly with 13(14) sts on each needle.

HEEL

Start to work heel by knitting the sts on needle I on to needle IV (26(28) sts for heel flap). Leave remaining sts on needles II and III. Turn work and start slip stitch pattern to reinforce heel:

Row 1 (WS): sl1 (with yarn at back of work), purl to end of row. Turn work.

Row 2 (RS): *sl1 (with yarn at back of work), k1*, repeat from * to * to end of row. Turn work.

Repeat rows 1 and 2 a total of 13(14) times and then work row 1 again (27(29) rows).

Start to work a French heel (rounded heel):

Row 1 (RS): sl1 (with yarn at back of work), k14(15), ssk, k1. Turn work.

Row 2 (WS): sl1 purlwise, p5, p2tog, p1. Turn work.

Row 3: sl1 knitwise, k6, ssk, k1. Turn work.

Row 4: sl1 purlwise, p7, p2tog, p1. Turn work.

Continue decreasing in this way, increasing the number of sts in the centre by one on each row until all sts at the sides have been decreased. Then work 1 more WS row. **Note:** for the larger size, there will be no stitch left to k1/p1 at the end of the row after the last decrease.

Turn work. Divide heel sts evenly between two needles with 8 sts on each needle. Knit sts on RH needle. This point (centre back) is now the start of the round.

FOOT

Knit the 8 sts on LH needle from heel (needle I). Using a spare needle, pick up 14(15) sts from LH edge of heel flap + 1 st between heel flap and needle II. Knit picked up sts on to needle I, turning sts knitwise. Knit sts on needle II and needle III. Using the needle with 8 sts on it, pick up 14(15) sts from RH edge of heel flap + 1 st between heel flap and needle III. Knit picked up sts and 8 sts from heel on to needle IV, turning picked up sts knitwise. You now have 72(76) sts.

Continue in stocking (stockinette) stitch, decreasing for gusset as follows: k2tog at end of needle I and ssk at beginning of needle IV. Repeat decreases on every alt round until there are 13(14) sts left on each needle.

Continue in stocking (stockinette) stitch until the foot of the sock measures approximately 20.5(22)cm / 8(8¾)in or covers the wearer's little toe.

Start to decrease to work a barn toe:

Needle I and needle III: work to last 3 sts, k2tog, k1.

Needle II and needle IV: k1, ssk, work to end.

Decrease as set on every alt round until there are 36 sts left and then work decreases on every round until there are 16 sts left.

Divide remaining sts evenly between two needles with 8 sts on the upper needle and 8 sts on the lower needle. Graft sts together. There are instructions and videos available online showing how to graft (sometimes called Kitchener stitch).

SECOND SOCK

Work the other sock in the same way.

FINISHING

Weave in ends. Carefully wet socks, place on a flat surface and block to measurements. Leave to dry. Steam block lightly if necessary.

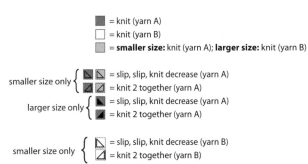

Chart

Work rounds 1–62(1–67)

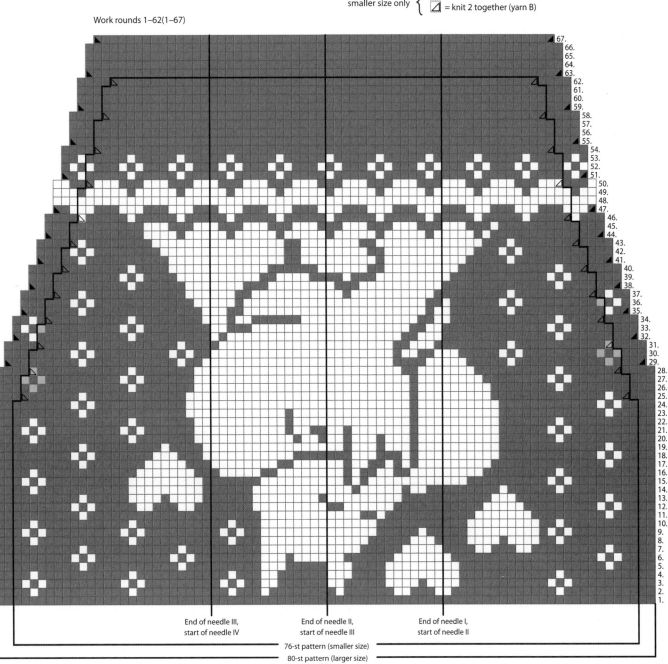

End of needle III, start of needle IV

End of needle II, start of needle III

End of needle I, start of needle II

76-st pattern (smaller size)

80-st pattern (larger size)

169

NIGHT AT SEA

Moominpappa gazes wistfully out to sea in these socks designed by Sonja Nykänen. These easy ankle-length socks are perfect as a beginner Fair Isle knitting project. The white crests of the waves, the ship's wheel and Moominpappa are embroidered in duplicate stitch later.

DESIGNER Sonja Nykänen

SIZE UK 4 (Europe 37, US Women's 6½, US Men's 5)

YARN

1 ball each of Novita Muumitalo (Moomin House) DK (8-ply/light worsted) yarn in Moomintroll 007 (A), The Groke 176 (B) and Snork 152 (C) and a small amount of Stinky 099 (D) for the embroidery; 100g/3½oz/225m/246yd

AMOUNT USED

50g (1¾oz) of yarns A and C, 100g (3½oz) of yarn B and 25g (1oz) of yarn D

KNITTING NEEDLES

3mm (UK 11, US 2/3) double-pointed needles or size to obtain correct tension (gauge)

TECHNIQUES

Twisted rib in the round:
knit 1 through back loop, purl 1, repeat from * to *.

Stocking (stockinette) stitch in the round:
Knit all rounds.

Fair Isle in the round:
Work in stocking (stockinette) stitch following chart and instructions. Catch in any floats longer than 3 sts by twisting the yarns around each other on the wrong side. Vary where you catch your floats in the design so they don't land in the same place on consecutive rounds.

TENSION (GAUGE) 25 sts in st st = 10cm (4in)

NOTE

The socks are worked top down from cuff to toe. Embroider the wheel, Moominpappa and the white tips of the waves once the socks are complete in duplicate stitch and backstitch.

LEG

Cast on 52 sts in yarn A and divide evenly between four needles with 13 sts on each needle. The start of the round is between needle I and needle IV at the back of the sock.

Join, being careful not to twist, and work 3cm (1¼in) in twisted rib in the round. Change to yarn B and knit 7cm (2¾in) in stocking (stockinette) stitch in the round.

Embroider the ship's wheel on the outside of the leg following Chart I in duplicate stitch. The design starts on round 5 after the rib. On the left sock, the centre stitch of the design is the first st of needle IV and on the right sock it is the last st of needle I.

Chart I

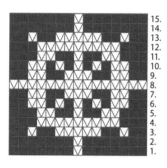

15.
14.
13.
12.
11.
10.
9.
8.
7.
6.
5.
4.
3.
2.
1.

▽ = embroider sts in duplicate stitch in yarn A

HEEL

Start to work heel by knitting the sts on needle I on to needle IV (26 sts for heel flap). Leave remaining sts on needles II and III. Turn work. K2, p22, k2. Turn work and start slip stitch pattern with a garter stitch edge to reinforce heel:

Row 1 (RS): k2 *sl1 (with yarn at back of work), k1*, repeat from * to * until last 2 sts, k2. Turn work.

Row 2 (WS): k2, purl until last 2 sts, k2. Turn work.

Repeat rows 1 and 2 a total of 13 times (26 rows).

Start to decrease to turn the heel:

Continue in the same slip stitch pattern as before to reinforce heel. Starting with a RS row, work in pattern until there are 9 sts left on LH needle, skpo and turn work.

Sl1 purlwise, purl 8 sts on WS until 9 sts remain on LH needle, p2tog and turn work. **Note:** there is no garter stitch at the edges now that the rows have become shorter.

Starting with a RS row, sl1 knitwise, work in pattern until there are 8 sts left on LH needle, skpo and turn work.

Continue as set working back and forth, i.e. always slip the first st of the row and skpo at the end of a RS row and p2tog at the end of a WS row. The number of sts at the sides will decrease by 1 each time, always leaving 10 sts in the centre. When you run out of side sts at the end of a WS row, k5 on RS. This point (centre back) is now the start of the round.

FOOT

Knit 5 sts on LH needle from heel (needle I). Using a spare needle, pick up 13 sts from LH edge of heel flap + 1 st between heel flap and needle II. Knit picked up sts on to needle I, turning sts knitwise. Knit sts on needle II and needle III. Using the needle with 5 sts on it, pick up 13 sts from RH edge of heel flap + 1 st between heel flap and needle III. Knit picked up sts and 5 sts from heel on to needle IV, turning picked up sts knitwise. You now have 64 sts.

Continue in stocking (stockinette) stitch, decreasing for gusset as follows: k2tog at end of needle I and skpo at beginning of needle IV. Work this decrease on every alt round until there are 52 sts left.

Then work in Fair Isle in stocking (stockinette) stitch following Chart II A: work rounds 1–3 of chart in Fair Isle, then work rounds 4–22 in stocking (stockinette) stitch in yarn C and then work rounds 23–25 in Fair Isle. **Note:** first work the white edges of the waves in yarn C. You will embroider them in duplicate stitch in yarn A afterwards. Work wave pattern in the area behind Moominpappa in yarns C and B in the same pattern as either side.

Work 6 rounds in stocking (stockinette) stitch in yarn B (rounds 26–31 of Chart II A) and then embroider the white tops of the waves and the top of Moominpappa as shown on chart.

Continue in stocking (stockinette) stitch and start to decrease to work a barn toe:

Needle I and needle III: work to last 3 sts, k2tog, k1.

Needle II and needle IV: k1, skpo, work to end.

Decrease as set on every alt round until there are 28 sts left. Now embroider the rest of the Moominpappa design following chart. Then repeat the toe decreases on every round until there are 8 sts left. Break yarn and thread through remaining sts.

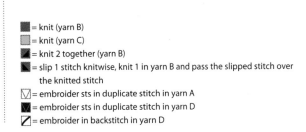

= knit (yarn B)

= knit (yarn C)

= knit 2 together (yarn B)

= slip 1 stitch knitwise, knit 1 in yarn B and pass the slipped stitch over the knitted stitch

= embroider sts in duplicate stitch in yarn A

= embroider sts in duplicate stitch in yarn D

= embroider in backstitch in yarn D

Chart II A

Work rounds 1–47

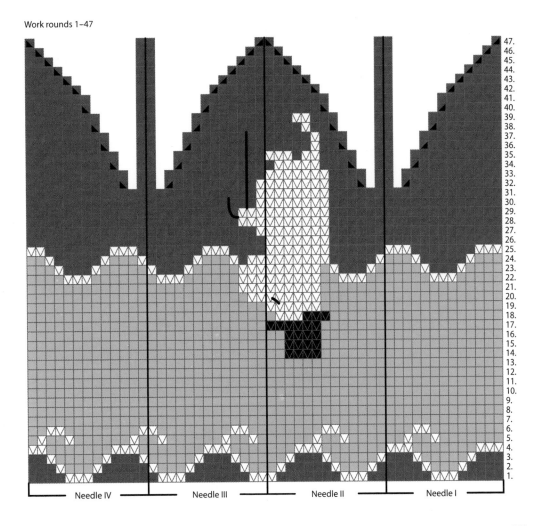

47.
46.
45.
44.
43.
42.
41.
40.
39.
38.
37.
36.
35.
34.
33.
32.
31.
30.
29.
28.
27.
26.
25.
24.
23.
22.
21.
20.
19.
18.
17.
16.
15.
14.
13.
12.
11.
10.
9.
8.
7.
6.
5.
4.
3.
2.
1.

Needle IV — Needle III — Needle II — Needle I

SECOND SOCK

Work the other sock in the same way but working the ship's wheel design on the other side following the instructions and embroidering the foot as shown in Chart II B.

FINISHING

Weave in ends. Carefully wet socks, place on a flat surface and block to measurements. Leave to dry. Steam gently under a cloth if necessary.

■ = knit (yarn B)
□ = knit (yarn C)
◤ = knit 2 together (yarn B)
◥ = slip 1 stitch knitwise, knit 1 in yarn B and pass the slipped stitch over the knitted stitch
▽ = embroider sts in duplicate stitch in yarn A
▼ = embroider sts in duplicate stitch in yarn D
╱ = embroider in backstitch in yarn D once sock is complete.

Chart II B

Work rounds 1–47

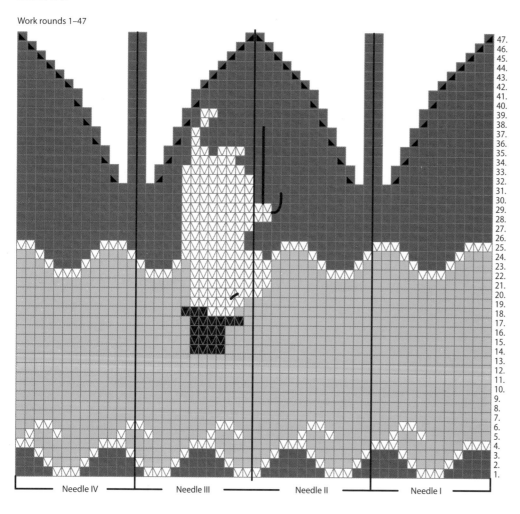

"'There are some things one can be absolutely sure of: sea currents, the seasons, the rising of the sun... And that lighthouses always work, too.'"

Moominpappa at Sea